WALLABY

D0059045

OTHER BOOKS
by
D. ROBERT WHITE

Look Homeward, Angel

King Lear

The Old Man and the Sea

The Brothers Karamazov

Blackstone's Commentaries on the Law

White's Law Dictionary*

*Soon to be published.

The Official Lawyer's Handbook

D. Robert White, Esq.

A Wallaby Book
Published by Simon & Schuster, Inc.
New York

Copyright © 1983 by D. Robert White, Esq.
Published by Wallaby Books
A Division of Simon & Schuster, Inc.
Simon & Schuster Building
1230 Avenue of the Americas
New York, New York 10020
Photos on pages 10, 42, 44, 63, 66–67, 161, 167, 171, 239, 240
copyright © WIDE WORLD PHOTOS
Designed by Judy Allan
WALLABY and colophon are registered trademarks of Simon & Schuster, Inc.
First Wallaby Books printing November 1983

10 9 8 7 6 5 4 3 2 1

Manufactured in the United States of America
Printed and bound by Command Web

Library of Congress Cataloging in Publication Data

White, D. Robert (Daniel Robert)
    The official lawyer's handbook.

    "A Wallaby book."
    1. Law—United States—Anecdotes, facetiae, satire,
etc. I. Title.
K184.W47   1983   340′.023′73   83-17494
ISBN: 0-671-47316-6

The Official Lawyer's Handbook has received universal acclaim:

"A masterpiece! If I had had the benefit of *The Official Lawyer's Handbook,* I could have come up with twenty or thirty commandments, easy."

—Moses

"Would that I could walk and talk with D. Robert White. He has mastered my method and then some."

—Socrates

"*The Official Lawyer's Handbook* is must reading for anyone who would forge a lasting empire."

—Justinian I

"I say D. Robert White can eat egg fu yong at my table any time."

—Confucius

"Legal writing at its best! Mr. White has demystified the sphinx of the law."

—Hammurabi

"I'm glad my *Commentaries* didn't have to compete with *The Official Lawyer's Handbook,* is all I can say."

—Sir William Blackstone

Acknowledgments

Many people assisted in producing *The Official Lawyer's Handbook,* voluntarily and unwittingly.

Martin J. Yudkowitz, J.D., Columbia, 1979, provided valuable encouragement and invaluable clever material. A funny guy who made a career mistake (see Chapter XV), Mr. Yudowitz's clients giggle all the way to the gallows.

Michael Goodman, J.D., University of Virginia, the exclusive cartoonist for the book, already has people referring to James Thurber as the Michael Goodman of his day.

Sincere thanks to John Freund and David Porter for their editorial and creative assistance and general know-how; to Professor of Law Phil Frickey and lawyers Randy Turk and David Wescoe, who contributed to several chapters; to lawyers Dan Attridge, Mary Ann Bernard, Jonathan Eddison, and Paul Glist, who offered helpful ideas; and to Jack Artenstein, Gene Brissie and Melissa Newman, who made things happen at Simon & Schuster.

Finally, special thanks to Dr. Laurie Adler, Dr. Nancy Petersmeyer, and Dr. Sibyl Wescoe for their psychiatric contributions, and to Dr. Dale Adler, my personal physician.

I am also grateful to Debbie Knopman and Ginger Mackay-Smith and to lawyers Missy Asbill Attridge, George Covington, Phil Frickey, Bill Hannaford, David Hayes, Liz Haile Hayes, Jamie Kaplan, Paul Pien, Jim Moody, Janet St. Amand, David Wescoe, and Chris Wright for allowing their pictures to appear in this book.

Dedication

This book is dedicated to Dad, my brother Ben, Aunt Mary, Uncle B.B., Uncle John, Granddad, Great Uncle Pettus, Cousin Pollard and all the other lawyers in my family.

Contents

Disasters
* *The Resumé*
* *Recruiting Letters*
(B) Recruiting Misrepresentations
(C) Hard Questions
* Understanding Billable Hours

(You can make it to the top . . . if you know what to kiss and whose)

Rule No. 1. **C.Y.A.** *(and seven other essential rules of survival)*

(The Crock at the End of the Rainbow)

*Spotting Lawyers Out
on the Town*

*(Latin and Other
Foreign Tongues)*

Introduction

Who among us has not at one time said, "Sue the bastard!" or "There ought to be a law . . ."?

The rub is that only lawyers know *how* to sue the bastard, or whether there *is* a law. If you, a non-lawyer, want to file a suit or find out about the law, you have to hire a lawyer—which, like hiring a prostitute, may be easy but not cheap.

A certain mystique surrounds the law. What do those guys study for three

"Before he went to law school he either agreed or disagreed with my opinions . . . now he concurs or dissents."

EIGHTEEN GOOD REASONS WHY YOU SHOULD BECOME A LAWYER
(Why not? Everyone else is.)

1. The money.

2. Your college major was English [History, Political Science, Celtic Folklore], which, along with a valid driver's license, may qualify you to drive a cab.

3. You think people who carry briefcases look important.

4. Your Uncle Herb is a lawyer.

5. You overslept on the morning of the business boards.

6. You're brilliant, you know it, and being a lawyer is one way to make sure everyone else knows it.

7. You want to reform the world.

8. You want to own the world.

9. You're Jewish and don't want to be a doctor.

10. You want to be a judge, because at present no one calls you "Your Honor."

11. The money.

12. You love to wear pin stripes but don't want to join the Mafia.

13. Ever since your electric train broke when you were in grade school, you've lived to sue the guy who sold it to you and break him financially.

14. You despise lawyers and want to be one so they can't jerk you around.

15. You're obsessed with the idea of an office and a dictaphone.

16. You think you could be a great courtroom advocate because you were a college debater and love to hear yourself talk.

17. You want to teach law because it's common knowledge that law professors have casual sex with their students.

18. The money.

years in law school? What are they saying when they approach the judge during a trial and whisper out of hearing of the jury? What are all those documents they always carry around? Why are they always talking in Latin?

This book tells all.

TEN HARD FACTS TO CONSIDER BEFORE CHOOSING A LEGAL CAREER
(Do you realize what those guys do?)

1. The average judge earns less than a plumber.

2. Everyone you know hates lawyers.

3. The thought of spending 80 percent of the rest of your life in an office behind a desk makes you want to up-chuck.

4. According to the Census Department, 78 percent of all lawyers are wider at the stomach than at the shoulders and resemble pears.

5. Criminal defense work is what interests you, but people charged with murder and rape are usually guilty as sin.

6. About a third of all lawyers have ulcers through which you could drive a Mack truck.

7. The number of lawyers who get jobs with established firms is about the same as the number who end up as short-order cooks—and the latter are happier.

8. A "light day" in a big firm runs from 8:30 A.M. to 7:30 P.M. A "light week" in a big firm consists of seven "light days."

9. The lawyers who spend the most time in court wear green suits and carry Naugahyde briefcases.

10. Probably not more than a third of all law professors have casual sex with their students.

"Can I at least keep the vest and briefcase?"

If you're thinking of becoming a lawyer or, sadly, are already committed to the task, this book will give you an edge in that highly competitive field.*

---

* There are already 610,000 lawyers in America, and last year over 110,000 people took the Law School Admission Test (not including an estimated 27,000 who showed up but left overcome by acute anxiety because they forgot their No. 2 pencils).

You don't want to spend your legal career chasing ambulances. You don't want your office to consist of the back seat of your '72 Vette (Chevette, that is) or the pay telephone booth at the Amoco station across from the courthouse.

You want to be a legal honcho—an adviser to presidents, sheiks, and chairmen of the board. You want a plush corner office, embossed stationery, a nice leather briefcase, and a secretary who'll screen United Way fund-raisers. This book tells you how.

This book walks you through every step of your legal career, from puberty to PARTNERSHIP. It gets you through that make-or-break first year of law school, providing enough key concepts and buzzwords to put you at the top of your class.

But this book is more than a ticket to success in law school. It's an *alternative* to law school, preparing you for a legal career better than any training you could get at Harvard or Columbia. It offers not only concepts, lingo, and training in the so-called "legal method," but also practical advice that would normally require years in the school of hard knocks. All this for less than six dollars.

Law schools are understandably hostile to this book: it renders them obsolete. As of this printing, seventeen state bar commissions are actively considering this book as a substitute for law school—which would not only advance the legal profession but also save you thousands of dollars and years of your life. (*See* chart.)

If you're already out of law school, this book is all the more critical. It shows you how to get into one of those high paying, white shoe firms, and, more difficult, how to survive once you're there.

This book is not designed just for lawyers, however. It is equally for "laymen"—that's what lawyers call the people they screw.

The legal profession is too important to remain veiled in secrecy. It pervades our existence. Whether you want to start a business, break a lease, make bail, or sue the doctor who told you the sex change operation was reversible, you need to know the law. To your utter distaste, you'll have to deal with a lawyer.

But you don't have to be at your lawyer's mercy, simply because right now you don't understand what he's up to. Dealing with him doesn't *have* to be like dealing with your doctor or your auto mechanic (who at least

ALTERNATIVE LEGAL EDUCATIONS: *YOU* MAKE THE CHOICE

Rank	Institution	Cost of Degree* (Estimated tuition, books and living expenses x 3 years)	Average Starting Salary*	Ratio Decidendi (Average starting salary/costs)
1	**The Official Lawyer's Handbook**	$ 5.95 (tax-deductible)	$36,500	6,134.45
2	Larry's Legal Institute of Duluth	$ 900	$ 2,600	2.88
3	University of Texas	$14,500	$24,500	1.69
4	U.C.L.A.	$22,000	$25,000	1.14
5	University of California at Berkeley	$28,500	$29,000	1.02
6	Columbia	$36,000	$33,500	.93
7	Georgetown	$30,000	$26,000	.87
8	University of Virginia	$29,500	$25,000	.85
9	Stanford	$39,500	$33,000	.84
10	University of Chicago	$39,000	$32,000	.82
11	Harvard	$41,500	$34,000	.82
12	Yale	$42,675	$35,000	.82
13	University of Michigan	$36,000	$29,000	.81
14	New York University	$39,000	$29,500	.76
15	University of Mississippi	$15,000	$12,000, 11 bags of corn and 43 "head" of chicken	Cannot be calculated

* Some of these figures were calculated from data provided by the schools indicated. Others were taken from secondary sources publicly available. Others were invented by the author. None should be relied upon other than to choose your life strategy.

give you a scar or a new carburetor to show for your money).

After reading this book, you'll know where your lawyer is coming from, how he got there, and just where "there" is.

You'll know what he does and why—and be able to protect yourself so he doesn't do it to you.

* * *

This book was written from the inside. Its author and various contributors are, to the eternal shame of our families, lawyers. Our composite resumé includes one former Supreme Court clerk and innumerable former clerks at the federal District and Circuit Court levels. It includes three editors-in-chief of Law Reviews that libraries actually stock.

The names of most of these contributors cannot appear even in Acknowledgments. As lawyers they know the importance of never confessing to anything. Those with families or large debts (the former include the latter) need to retain their jobs, and the legal profession is not yet able to laugh at itself.

For our protection, we hereby declare that all characters portrayed directly or indirectly in this book are fictional. Any resemblance to living persons is coincidental and, for them, presumably, embarrassing in the extreme.

I.

Determining Your Legal Quotient

(IS YOUR MIND A STEEL TRAP . . . OR A JAR OF MARSHMALLOW FLUFF?)

Not everyone is cut out for a legal career. Before commencing the legal equivalency training in this book, take the following self-assessment quiz to determine whether you have the "right stuff" for the law. You might discover that you really aren't suited to it at all—better to find out now, before your vocabulary is permanently encrusted with Latin. You might also discover, if your score is too high, that you aren't suited to anything else—in which case this book could prove to be the best investment of your life. (Answers and a grading scale appear on page 12.)

LEGAL QUOTIENT EXAM

1. When you wake up each day, the first thing you do is:

(a) Hit the snooze control.

(b) Make the bed, polish your shoes to a high gloss, brush your teeth to a high gloss, and recite five sections of the Internal Revenue Code —all before breakfast.

(c) Turn on the afternoon news, to see what you missed that morning.

(d) Wonder where you are and who's beside you.

2. If your boss told you that you would have to spend the next two weeks proofreading the Encyclopedia Britannica, you would:

(a) Reply that you don't see any reason why you couldn't complete the job by next Monday.

(b) Tell him you'd love to undertake so significant and interesting a project, but just yesterday you heard Hayes down the hall saying he dreams of such an assignment, and you'd be willing to defer to Hayes on this occasion.

(c) Grimace but resign yourself to the task.

(d) Lose your lunch on the spot.

3. When you were a child, you experienced lust in the presence of:

(a) Your parent of the opposite sex.

(b) Your parent of the same sex.

(c) Either parent's briefcase.

(d) Your Great Dane Gaylord.

4. *Word association.* The first thing that comes to your mind when you hear the word *prison* is:

(a) Violent criminals.

(b) Potential clients.

(c) Law school.

(d) Limited liability.

(e) I.R.S. audit.

5. When you used to watch Perry Mason, you rooted for:

(a) Hamilton Burger.

(b) Warren Burger.

(c) Della.

Perry Mason—a Lawyer's Lawyer.

(d) Perry.

(e) Ironside.

6. When a sexual opportunity presents itself, you:

(a) Plunge in headlong, so to speak, without concern for the future.

(b) Inquire first whether s/he is married, is on some form of birth control, and has recently experienced anything resembling cold sores.

(c) Require a signed "palimony" disclaimer.

(d) Are too stunned to act.

7. *Word association.* The first thing that comes to your mind when you hear the word *security* is:

(a) Blanket.

(b) Police lock.

(c) Malpractice insurance.

(d) A comfort letter from Cravath, Swaine & Moore.

8. Your idea of a great time is:

(a) A late night proofreading franchise contracts at the office.

(b) Foreclosing a mortgage on a widow with six kids.

(c) Around-the-clock negotiations on a new labor contract.

(d) Nothing remotely resembling any of the above.

9. Your favorite color is:

(a) Mahogany

(b) Kelly green.

(c) Long green.

(d) Yellow, preferably 8½ x 13 with narrow margins.

10. When you think of lawyers, you envision people who:

(a) Protect the downtrodden.

(b) Screw the proletariat.

(c) Couldn't get jobs in productive sectors of society.

(d) You try not to think about lawyers.

11. The first thing that comes to your mind when you look at the following ink blot is:

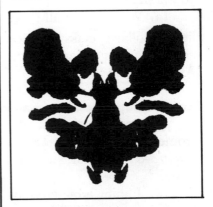

(a) The Jackson Pollock in your firm's main conference room.

(b) A hit-and-run victim (and potential client).

(c) The insanity defense.

(d) Prefer to research the issue before commenting.

12. If you were to drive over a dog that had darted into the street, your first impulse would be to:

(a) Feel concern that it

may still be alive and suffering.

(b) Roll up your window.

(c) Try to locate the owner, to express your regret.

(d) Try to locate the owner, to demand payment for the dent in your grill.

(e) Back up and go over it again, to teach it a lesson.

13. During idle moments you fantasize about:

(a) Winning a multi-million dollar class action against the American Medical Association.

(b) Oral arguments before the Supreme Court.

(c) Oral acts with the women you saw in the *Sports Illustrated* summer swimsuit issue.

(d) Joining a big-city law firm, so you wouldn't have to worry about any more idle moments.

14. Which of the following do you consider most likely to guarantee success in the law?

(a) A precise, analytical mind.

(b) Thirty charcoal gray suits with vests.

(c) A good word processor.

(d) This book.

Quiz Answers

1. (a) 6, (b) 2, (c) 1, (d) 0
2. (a) 7, (b) 3, (c) 1, (d) 0
3. (a) 1, (b) 0, (c) 6, (d) 2
4. (a) 2, (b) 6, (c) 0, (d) 5, (e) 1
5. (a) 4, (b) 0, (c) 1, (d) 2, (e) 0
6. (a) 1, (b) 0, (c) 2, (d) 6
7. (a) 0, (b) 1, (c) 7, (d) 2
8. (a) 5, (b) 7, (c) 1, (d) 0
9. (a) 2, (b) 0, (c) 3, (d) 7
10. (a) 2, (b) 3, (c) 1, (d) 0
11. (a) 0, (b) 6, (c) 3, (d) 7
12. (a) 0, (b) 1, (c) 2, (d) 6, (e) 3
13. (a) 1, (b) 2, (c) 4, (d) 7
14. (a) 2, (b) 4, (c) 6, (d) 7

Evaluating Your Results

If you scored:

Between 65 and 93:

Congratulations (sort of). You're compulsive, calculating, avaricious, and no doubt already too blind to go out without a dog. You could make a real name for yourself in the law.

Between 45 and 64:

Not bad. You have the makings of a lawyer, maybe even partnership material. Sometimes you let your feelings for humanity interfere with your professional role, but with work you could learn to repress these feelings.

Between 20 and 44:

Hey—so you're not going to be the next F. Lee Bailey. You're a likeable person with a bright life ahead. Enjoy!

Between 0 and 20:

You've gone too far the other way. You're a weak-kneed, mealy-mouthed jellyfish, with no gumption. Straighten up and try to make something of yourself—but not in the law.

II

Getting into the Right Law School

("MY ROOMMATE THE MOONIE SCORED IN THE 98TH PERCENTILE ON THE LSAT AND GOT INTO HARVARD. WHY DIDN'T I?")

Neither law schools nor their admissions officers care about the *whole* person. Law school isn't college. It isn't out to mold you into a better human being, or to prepare you for life. It doesn't care whether any of your classmates will like you.

Sure, you swam the English channel in ski boots, and you play classical ukulele. You managed the varsity jazzercize team, and you were the first male in your school's history to play Lady Macbeth. But law schools need more Junior Achievers

The ivy-covered halls of the Harvard Law School. (Photo by Christopher Morrow)

like the Titanic needed more ice machines.

Law Schools look at two factors: grades and LSAT scores. They just plug the figures into a formula and take as many applicants as they have room for (discounted by the number of people who will die, go to other schools, or decide there must be a less painful way to gird one's loins for life).

Sir William Blackstone—would his LSAT score get him into law school today?

What about those stupid essays and recommendations required by the application? These should be viewed more as obstacles than opportunities.

Your essays could show you to be barely literate, not-withstanding your *magna cum laude* English thesis at Princeton: "Over 100 Really Good Knock, Knock Jokes." Your recommendations might say only that your methadone treatment appears to be working and your parole officer thinks well of you.

If you're an undergraduate determined to go to law school, your best strategy is to go for the highest grades and LSAT scores you can get. There may be some well-rounded, likeable people in law school, but that isn't what got them in.

THE LAW SCHOOL ADMISSION TEST (LSAT)

There is ongoing debate as to what the LSAT measures beyond your ability to come up with the $40.00 to register and several No. 2 pencils. Nevertheless, experience shows that two factors may significantly enhance your performance during the hour of truth: (1) familiarity with the style of LSAT ques-

tions, and (2) a good supply of anti-diuretics. The latter can be obtained at any drug store. The former can be had from the following sample questions.

Sample LSAT Questions

I. *Reading Comprehension*

Directions:
Read each passage below and answer the questions following each passage by blackening the space beside the answer you believe is most nearly correct.

1. "It was the best of times, it was the worst of times, it was the age of wisdom, it was the age of foolishness . . . [read the novel *A Tale of Two Cities,* attached to your exam booklet] . . . it is a far, far better rest that I go to than I have ever known."

Question: In the above story, what time it is?
- ☐ (a) The best of times.
- ☐ (b) The worst of times.
- ☐ (c) The New York Times.
- ☐ (d) About 2:00 o'clock.

2. "Know thyself."
Question: In the above passage, the writer is
- ☐ (a) Quoting Plato.
- ☐ (b) Advocating a solipsistic approach to epistemology.
- ☐ (c) Employing an archaic usage.
- ☐ (d) Describing your social life.

II. *Analytical Reasoning*

Directions:
In this section you are given a question based on a stated set of conditions. Choose the best answer and mark the corresponding space beside that answer.

1. Einstein's theory of relativity postulated that there can be no motion at a speed greater than that of light in a vacuum, and time is dependent on the relative motion of an observer measuring the time. If a hydrogen atom electron is accelerated at a rate of π^2/speed of light through an inverse hypermagnetic positron field and then bombarded with neutrons in a nuclear pile critical core reaction, what time is it?
- ☐ (a) The best of times.
- ☐ (b) The worst of times.
- ☐ (c) About 2:00 o'clock.
- ☐ (d) Time to think about business school.

2. For a dinner party, Missy must prepare several different three-bean salads, using chili beans, wax beans, lima beans, kidney beans, and garbanzos. Note that (1) chili beans and lima beans do not taste good together,

and (2) lima beans and garbanzos do not look good together.

Missy can prepare how many salads of the following types:

☐ (a) Nine that resemble the bottom of a bird cage.

☐ (b) Four that will have her guests exchanging embarrassed glances within ten minutes.

☐ (c) Two that her pet goat would not eat.

☐ (d) None of the above—if you want to be a bean counter, take the CPA exam.

III. *Logical Reasoning*

Directions:
In this section you are required to evaluate the reasoning of the following passage. Although more than one choice may appear correct, use common sense and reasonableness to select the *best* answer. Then mark the appropriate space.

1. If Mr. Smith is a member of Club A, and Ms. Johnson is a member of Club B, and Mr. Smith and Ms. Wilson are members of Club C, and no members of Club B who are also members of Club A are women who belong to the same club as men who belong to more than one club, *then*

☐ (a) Mr. Smith is a lesbian.

☐ (b) Club B must be in California.

☐ (c) Mr. Smith lied to get into Club C.

☐ (d) About 2:00 o'clock.

2. Ramona said, "All dogs bark. This animal does not bark. Therefore this animal is not a dog."
Which of the following most closely parallels the logic of this statement?

☐ (a) Cats do not bark. Cats climb trees. Trees have bark.

☐ (b) Lawyers overcharge. Taxi meters overcharge. Lawyers are taxi meters.

☐ (c) George sells cars. Every car sold by George is poorly built. George is a Chrysler dealer.

☐ (d) Dogs bay at the moon. Your dates bay at the moon. You would be better off getting to know thyself.

IV. *Evaluation of Facts*

Directions:

This section consists of a set of rules followed by a factual situation. You are required to apply the rules to the facts, blackening the space beside the answers that best reflect the apparent meaning of the rules.

Rules. The offense of first degree murder consists of two elements: (1) a deadly act against a victim, and (2) an intent to commit the deadly act.

Factual Situation. Mr. Jones enters Sydney's Unisex Barbershop in a tough section of New York City. While he is waiting for a haircut, an employee of Sydney's Unisex Barbershop sees him and, believing him to be someone else, runs a chain saw through the upper half of his head.

Question. On trial for first degree murder, the employee of Sydney's

Unisex Barbershop should be found:

- ☐ (a) Clearly guilty of taking too much off the top.
- ☐ (b) Not guilty because of assumption-of-risk principles re-specting unisex barbershops.
- ☐ (c) Guilty but nevertheless a suitable candidate for mayor of Chicago.
- ☐ (d) About 2:00 o'clock.

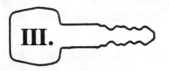

III.

Law School

("ARE YOU TELLING ME SOCRATES DID IT THIS WAY?")

(A) THE LAW SCHOOL EXPERIENCE

Legal lore describes the law school experience thus:

In the first year they scare you to death.

In the second year they work you to death.

In the third year they bore you to death.

This is roughly true.

The most memorable aspect of the *first* year—fear—is the result of the "Socratic method" of instruction, or "learning through humiliation."

The overwork in the *second* year is the result of insecurity. Based on their first-year grades, only 10 per-cent of the class now ranks in the top 10 percent of the class. But 100 percent of the class is *used* to ranking in the top 10 percent. The people who now rank in the bottom 90 percent feel confused and insecure. They channel these feelings into hard work.

The boredom in the *third* year is something you would have noticed in the first year if you hadn't been so scared.

Law school has been described as a place for the accumulation of learning. First-year students bring some in; third-year students take none away. Hence it accumulates.

The Socratic Method
(Is hemlock the only escape?)

The most talked-about aspect of the law school experience, featured prominently in *The Paper Chase, One L* and *Apocalypse Now,* is the "Socratic method" of instruction. Designed to convey not bare information but the legal *method* of analysis, it involves an exchange or dialogue between the professor and a randomly chosen student, with the student pressed to answer ever deeper levels of questions regarding the case of the day.

The Socratic method is highly controversial. Its potential pedagogic value indisputably surpasses that of the old-fashioned lecture methods, which caused even the most diligent students to experience symptoms of narcolepsy. In practice, its shortcomings are severe.

First, few professors are adept in its use. The skills of a few recognized masters— Arthur Miller of Harvard, Benno Schmidt of Columbia, Raymond Goetz of U. Kansas, Socrates of Athens— cannot offset the ineptness of those who waste innumerable class hours in dialogues like the following:

Professor Brager:
"Mr. Cobb, are you with us today?"

Student Cobb:
(raising hand):
"Here."

Professor Brager:
"Then let us proceed. What am I thinking?"

Student Cobb:
"I beg your pardon?"

Professor Brager:
"What thought is passing through my mind at this moment?"

Student Cobb:
"Uh . . . I don't exactly know . . . it could be anything . . . that is . . . I'm not . . ."

Professor Brager:
"Mr. Cobb, did you manage to overlook the assignment I gave at the end of class yesterday?"

Student Cobb:
"No, I read it . . . twice, in fact. It had to do with the Supreme Court's interpretation of Section 805(b) of the National Labor Relations Act."

Professor Brager:
"If you've read it, as you *claim*, why are you

unable to answer a simple question regarding the NLRA?"

The other practical problem with the Socratic method is that professors who are either lazy or uninterested in teaching use it to kill class time without having to prepare a lecture:

Professor Ryan:
"Ms. Bond, what did you think of the cases assigned for today?"
Student Bond:
"All of them? They seemed fine, I guess. Are you thinking of any one in particular?"
Professor Ryan:
"Take any one you like. Did you agree or disagree with it?"
Student Bond:
"Well, there was *one* I can think of that I agreed with."
Professor Ryan:
"Okay. Uh, let's see . . . Mr. Feder, did you agree or disagree with the case to which Ms. Bond is referring?"
Student Feder:
"I'm not sure. Which one is she referring to?"

Professor Ryan:

"Ms. Bond, please explain the case to which you're referring to Mr. Feder."

This sort of thing is a far cry from the system that produced Plato. If Socrates were alive today he'd be turning over in his grave.

*   *   *

Just because a professor calls on you doesn't mean you have to answer. If he doesn't know you personally or have a seating chart with pictures, you can simply remain silent (the "foxhole technique"), pretending you're not there. The only problem with this technique is that students who know you may give you away by glancing in your direction. If this happens, turn and stare at the person sitting beside you.

(B) LAW STUDENTS AND LAW PROFESSORS (The Good, the Bad and the Criminally Ugly)

Law students have to learn to deal with two sets of people: classmates and law professors. The former have to be dealt with because they're physically ubiquitous: in the classroom, at the campus cafeteria, on that obscure library sofa where you were hoping to take a nap. The latter have to be dealt with because they're *psychologically* omnipresent, constantly hovering about like parental superegos that talk in Latin. If you're planning to go to law school, you need to know about both groups.

Classmates

Although your law school classmates will come in all sizes, colors, pedigrees, and sexes, they will fall into easily identifiable categories.

1. The Mainstreamer.

Most of your classmates will have proceeded directly from college to law school and will be planning to go directly into private practice—sort of like the great Tinkers-to-Evers-to-Chance double-play combination, only here it's B.A. to J.D. to C.A.S.H.

Some will have chosen this path out of driving ambition; others will have been forced into it by their parents (who couldn't bear the thought of breaking a seven-generation succession of lawyers); most will have done it because they didn't have anything else to do.*

The Mainstreamer is easily recognizable. If male, his dress is conventional, his hair length short, his politics middle-of-the-road, and his drug habits mild. If female, her dress is conventional, her politics mildly feminist, her parents somewhat anxious about her future, and her willingness to engage in premarital sex dependent upon whether the relationship is "meaningful."

By and large, you will be able to understand and enjoy these people. The odds are that you are one of them.

---

* "Unlike medicine, few young people decide to be lawyers early in life. Instead, law schools have traditionally been the refuge of able, ambitious college seniors who cannot think of anything else they want to do." Derek C. Bok, President, Harvard University, "A Flawed System" in *Harvard Magazine* 38, 70 (May-June 1983).

2. The Grad School Burnout.

A number of your classmates will have spent time working on other graduate degrees before going into law. Usually the Grad School Burnout switched fields out of simple necessity: she abandoned Hobbes for Holmes, Blake for Blackstone, and Proust for Prosser because she was in the habit of eating.

The Grad School Burnout has a hint of pathos about her, because she sees all too clearly that what would have been the next generation of philosophers, historians, and scientists has been transmogrified into an army of litigators, patent attorneys, and municipal bond specialists. Don't feel too sorry for the Grad School Burnout, however: she may be broke, but she represents strong competition.

3. The Computerhead.

The primary distinguishing feature of the Computerhead is that his undergraduate major was physics, engineering or some other "hard science." You

The Computerhead

can still recognize him by his thick glasses and the pocket calculator that he keeps strapped to his waist—even when he sleeps.

In college, travelling under the label of Nerd, the Computerhead hung around the computer center on Saturday nights to meet women. He did this for four years, even though he never met any.

4. The Flamer.

Flamers, known in some schools as Gunners, are the most conspicuous as well as the most objectionable feature of law school. Flamers will have their hands in the air throughout all classes, manually pleading for an opportunity to discuss arcane points of law discovered in unrequired reading. At the end of each class they will bolt from their seats (consistently front and center) to the podium, where they will collar the professor and further attempt to display their mastery of the obscure.

The psychology of the Flamer is pitiable. Deeply anxious and insecure, he degrades himself regularly with brown-nosing of authority figures—not just professors but law librarians, weekend security guards, and the director of campus food services. The important fact for you to remember is that the Flamer's tactics reflect his internal necessities, *not* the realities of the law school situation. The Flamer is no more likely to get good grades than you are.

You cannot always ignore the Flamer; his excesses force their way into your life. But you should resist the temptation to stitch a dog muzzle to his face. Professors know how to deal with Flamers, having encountered them before; Flamers are as old as the law.

Law Professors

Law professors are a proudly idiosyncratic lot. Being as weird as you want to be is a major perk of academia, and some law professors make Andy Warhol look conventional. Nevertheless, like their students, law professors fall into identifiable categories.

1. The National Expert.

Most law faculties have at least one National Expert, someone whose name is associated across the land with a given subject—*Powell on Property, Williston on Contracts, Yudkowitz on Brain Death.*

There is only a chance correlation, if any, between status as a National Expert and competence as a teacher. The National Expert didn't get where he is by devoting his time to teaching. His lectures consist of "cases I have won" and "Supreme Court Justices I call by their first names."

Many National Experts are wealthy. Those with expertise in tax, securities, or other commercial areas maintain lucrative consulting practices in the "one day per week" to which their teaching contracts purport to restrict such activities.

National Experts in noncommercial areas such as civil procedure or criminal law convert their expertise into new BMW's by publishing $47.50 casebooks that their classes are required to purchase.

2. The Fuzzhead.

Some professors specialize in areas of notable obscurity. The Fuzzhead teaches undersubscribed seminars on "Noise Regulation," "Navajo Tribal Law," or "Liquidated Damages in China During the Ming Dynasty."

The Fuzzhead (possibly a Computerhead in law school) may be brilliant, but the same escapist impulses that got him into his area of expertise render him unable to relate to other creatures that walk on two legs. He is a consistently miserable teacher, particularly when re-quired to teach mainstream courses such as "Contracts" or "Evidence." He should be avoided unless he is an easy grader—or unless you are of the Fuzzhead ilk yourself.

3. The Old Curmudgeon.

The Old Curmudgeon is a classic feature of the law school landscape. Sometimes a former National Expert grown irascible in his twilight years, he is dogmatic, demanding, impatient, crotchety and semi-surly—the life of any party.

The Old Curmudgeon

conducts his classes as would a drill sergeant: you *will* attend all of his classes, you *will* be in your seat when he arrives at the beginning of each class, you *will* be prepared to discuss any assigned case.

The only way to deal with the Old Curmudgeon is craven capitulation. If he accuses you of inadequate preparation, shamefacedly apologize. If he charges you with genetic idiocy, lament your forebears' tradition of inbreeding.

Take comfort in the knowledge that the humiliation you risk by entering his class each day is no greater than that risked by each of your classmates. Take additional comfort in the knowledge that the Old Curmudgeon may not last another semester.

4. The Young Star.

Law school faculties are in constant search of the Young Star, someone short on years but long on the right credentials. Usually a former Supreme Court clerk and Law Review Editor-in-Chief, the true Young Star confirms his Young Stardom by early publication of a highly acclaimed article or treatise, one noted for its "fresh outlook," "novel insights," and red binding.

The Young Star is a colorful figure on the law school campus, with his longish hair, grubby clothes, longshoreman's vocabulary, and self-rolled funny cigarettes at parties. Also colorful are his apocalyptic analyses of society. The only people who agree with these analyses are undergraduates, but their support is sincere.

5. The Deadwood.

Every law student faculty has a few tenured members who don't do anything. In this respect law school faculties resemble private firms.

Although not necessarily elderly, Deadwoods don't write articles, don't serve on law reform committees, don't engage in private consulting, and apparently don't prepare for their classes. No one is sure what Deadwoods do with their time. Rumor has it that some of them have very nice gardens.

6. The Entertainer.

Many law professors pride themselves on being entertaining. Some think they could stand in for Johnny Carson. A few could. Because it is more fun to be entertained than bored as you sit in class, you will appreciate the Entertainer's wit.

The problem with the Entertainer is that students are often lulled by his levity into thinking he is an easy grader, only to get their socks blown off by the final exam. Enjoy the Entertainer, but don't slack up in his class any more than in your others. Tape your socks up for his final exam.

(C) LAW SCHOOL IN A NUTSHELL: THE HORNBOOK'S HORNBOOK

For at least the first two years of law school, law students are obsessed with their courses. They spend every waking hour trying to ingest, in regurgitable form, everything there is to know about so-called "core" subjects in the law.*

---

* Many students attempt to ingest these materials at the same time they are ingesting their breakfast or lunch. Not only is this bad for your digestion, but dried corn flakes and peanut butter on your textbooks substantially reduce their resale value.

Students also study a number of obscure subjects (Cow Law; Law of the Banana), either to pad their schedules or because they go to Yale and that's all that was offered.

But the core subjects dominate the curriculum in the first year, and they're all that a practicing lawyer needs to know. The following sections set forth all the concepts and buzzwords of the core subjects, in clearer form than you'd ever get them in law school.

**CONTRACTS
(The Ties That Bind)**

A passing familiarity with the law of contracts is all you need to hold yourself out as a "commercial" lawyer. Leases, security agreements, trust indentures and lots of other documents with high falutin' names are just con-tracts. This is good to know if another lawyer presents you with some document and you have no idea what it is. If it requires signing, and it isn't a will or something that has to be filed in court, you can call it a "contract" without fear of being laughed at.

Offer and Acceptance

The entire law of contracts can be summed up in two words: offer and acceptance (well, three words).

An offer is just what it sounds like:
"Hey Baby, $50.00 for some action?"

So is an acceptance:
"Sure. Your place or mine?"

Whether a contract has been formed depends on whether there has been a "meeting of the minds." The acceptance must "match" the offer.

Dan offers to take Anne to an expensive place for dinner if she'll accompany him to the prom on Saturday night. Anne replies, "Not on your life, spittoon face."

Here there has been no meeting of the minds. Anne's reply did not "match" Dan's offer. No contract was formed.

Offers and acceptances can be "conditional":

Andy: "I'd like to take you to the prom on Saturday night—*as long as* your face doesn't break out."

Betty-Jo: "Okay—*Unless* someone else on the football team asks me to go."

Consideration

Complicating the law of contracts is the concept of "consideration." The law will not enforce just any promise. For example, it will not enforce a promise to make a gift: "In two years, I won't want this toothbrush anymore. Then it's yours." It will enforce only those promises given in exchange for some return promise or equivalent sacrifice. This return promise or sacrifice constitutes the "consideration" supporting the enforceability of the contract.

No one understands this concept. Why they call it "consideration," when it has nothing to do with being nice to someone, is one of the law's well shrouded mysteries.

Nevertheless, at least nominal consideration always has to be there. According to law school lore, the delivery of a mere peppercorn would be sufficient consideration for a contract to transfer the Empire State Building, complete with Fay Wray and a large hairy doorman who swats airplanes. This is why even multi-billion dollar contracts may start out with a bizarre recital: "For $1.00 and other valuable *consideration*. . . ." At the closing of the deal one of the lawyers may actually present the other with a $1 bill (promptly recording it and billing it to the client with interest).

Breach

What if your client breaches a contract? What if *you* breach a contract? Should either of you be embarrassed about it?

The answer to the last question is no. In some instances the law *wants* you to breach your contract. Let's say you've entered a contract to build a house for someone on a piece of land that turns out to have water two feet below the surface. The ground is so soft you couldn't pitch a boy scout tent on it, much less a building.

Do you have to proceed according to plan, however futile it may be? No. The law doesn't see any point in your going broke, getting upset, and having your face break out because of this one contract.

All the law would require in such a case is that you give the other fellow enough money to "make him whole" (read "give him whatever a jury feels he ought to have"). A jury would take into account such factors as the cost of building the house elsewhere, whether either party knew about the water underneath the dirt, and the race and sex of the persons involved.

Unenforceable Contracts

The law won't enforce certain categories of contracts, regardless of the presence of consideration, the absence of breach, or anything else. One of these categories consists of contracts that are "contrary to public policy." Shylock's pound-of-flesh bargain would not be enforced north of the Mason-Dixon line today (southern jurisdictions remain very strict), and most courts would not require the loser of a bet on the Notre Dame-Ohio State football game to run three times naked around the Ohio State stadium shouting "Woody Hayes for President!"

Essentially the same is true for contracts made under duress. A court would not require you to perform a contract that you accepted after a fellow whose last name ends in a vowel made you an offer you couldn't refuse. Of course, few such contracts actually make it to court, and there's no predicting how a judge will rule after receiving an "offer" to go swimming in the East River in a cement bathing suit.

A final category of unenforceable contracts exists by virtue of the doctrine of "unconscionability." Occasionally a judge decides that a contract is so unfair, so grossly one-sided, as to be unconscionable, and he'll be damned if he'll enforce it. The underlying theory is that no sober person would sign such a contract, and the stronger party must have somehow duped the weaker party.

A classic case in this area involved a couple who bought a Plymouth from an auto dealer in New Jersey. The bill of sale carried a disclaimer—in print so tiny it could be read only with an electron microscope—saying that neither the dealer nor Chrysler would be liable for bodily injuries resulting from defects in the car. Supposedly the couple were stuck with that contract, but when the steering wheel came off in the hands of the wife ten days later, she sued.

The court ruled for the wife, saying the contract was unconscionable. He said that the average consumer has too little bargaining power in relation to the automobile giants, and the public interest in preventing bodily harm weighs against enforcing this kind of deal.

Liberal professors hail this ruling as a victory for the common man. Conservative professors denounce it as another example of judges venting their sexual frustrations on the productive elements of society.

The liberals are right. This contract was unconscionable. It wasn't made between two intelligent, rational, free-acting parties. No one in his right mind would buy a Plymouth from an auto dealer in New Jersey.

The preceding case doesn't mean you shouldn't include hundreds of unconscionable, illegible and unreadable disclaimers in the contracts you draft for your retailing clients. These provisions serve the important "dust in the eyes" function, blinding the consumer to his actual rights.

Go ahead and include a clause saying the purchaser acknowledges having test-driven the car, inspected the spare tire, and counted the spark plugs, even though he won't have known to do so. Throw in a clause saying the purchaser acknowledges having supervised the assembly of his stereo system, even though it was put together in

Taiwan. Throw in a clause saying the purchaser acknowledges having tested the video game on the premises of the store, even though he's an invalid who hasn't left his home in years.

The consumer won't be able to *find* these clauses, much less know how to strike them out. When he comes back to complain that the car has no spark plugs, the stereo has no sound, and the Pac Man on his video game throws up every time it eats a power pill, you can point them out to him, and he won't know they aren't worth the paper they're printed on.

PALIMONY—A TRAP FOR THE UN-WEARY

Except in a few special situations, contracts need not be in writing to be enforceable. In some instances, contracts need not even be spoken to be enforceable—a court may find an "implied contract" based on the conduct of the parties.

Such contracts have received substantial publicity in recent years with the rise of "palimony" suits, usually involving an action brought by a woman against her former lover, claiming breach of an implied contract of support.

There are no statutes addressing this issue; it's a social question, one that turns on the mores of the day. What *are* the legitimate expectations of a woman who accepts an invitation to move in with a man for a couple of years? Has he necessarily promised her support for life? What if he invites her to stay over for a single evening—has he at least promised to buy her brunch the next day?

What if the tables are turned—she's a rich neurologist, and he's a starving artist who moves into *her* apartment?

Does the whole thing depend on whether they had sexual relations? Is his case better if he can prove he's impotent?

It is difficult to counsel clients in this area, both because the law is in flux and because no would-be Lothario interrupts his passions to consult his lawyer regarding potential liability. For the present the best course is to supply lecherous clients of both sexes with blank disclaimers (a sample is set forth below), which they should have their prospective lovers execute at the first sign of lust.

————

Date: ____

PALIMONY WAIVER

The undersigned prospective lover (the "Lover"), being of sound mind, nubile body, and substantial libidinal urges, hereby acknowledges the mutual nature of all pleasures and gratifications accruing from any prior or future carnal relations, consummated or otherwise, between the undersigned and (your name)_____
(such carnal relations and all pleasures and gratifications accruing therefrom referred to hereinafter as "Lust"), and hereby waives and disclaims any right or entitlement to pecuniary or other benefits presently owing in connection with, or hereafter arising from, said Lust.

_____
(Prospective Lover)

Witness: I hereby attest to the accuracy of the representations set forth hereinabove, having witnessed all or substantial portions of said Lust, in person or on films.

_____
(Witness)

CIVIL PROCEDURE
(Avoiding the Merits of a Case)

If you want to be a trial lawyer, you need to know about civil procedure. Civil procedure covers the rules of court you must follow when suing someone or being sued. The word "civil" has nothing to do with politeness; it differentiates the rules that apply to a "civil" action from those that apply to a "criminal" action. The latter is what you'll face in most places if you stab someone, or if you jaywalk in Washington, D. C.

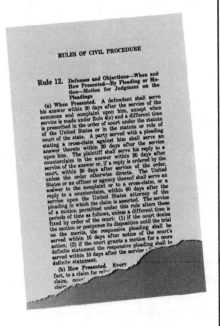

RULES OF CIVIL PROCEDURE

Rule 12. Defenses and Objections—When and How Presented—By Pleading or Motion—Motion for Judgment on the Pleadings

(a) When Presented. A defendant shall serve his answer within 20 days after the service of the summons and complaint upon him, except when service is made under Rule 4(e) and a different time is prescribed in the order of court under the statute of the United States or in the statute or rule of court of the state. A party served with a pleading stating a cross-claim against him shall serve an answer thereto within 20 days after the service upon him. The plaintiff shall serve his reply to a counterclaim in the answer within 20 days after service of the answer or, if a reply is ordered by the court, within 20 days after service of the order, unless the order otherwise directs. The United States or an officer or agency thereof shall serve an answer to the complaint or to a cross-claim, or a reply to a counterclaim, within 60 days after the service upon the United States attorney of the pleading in which the claim is asserted. The service of a motion permitted under this rule alters these periods of time as follows, unless a different time is fixed by order of the court: (1) if the court denies the motion or postpones its disposition until the trial on the merits, the responsive pleading shall be served within 10 days after notice of the court's action; (2) if the court grants a motion for a more definite statement the responsive pleading shall be served within 10 days after the service of the more definite statement.

(b) How Presented. Every fact, to a claim for relief, claim, coun' claim

There are four basic concepts you need to understand about civil procedure.

Standing

"Standing" refers to a concrete, personal interest in a particular lawsuit. It's something you're required to have in order to stay in court. Such an interest is easy to prove when you've been run over by a truck. Your injuries constitute your interest. Your broken legs give you standing.

But what if you want to sue Congress for passing a law restricting fat people from walking on public sidewalks during the lunch hour? If you're skinny, say, 6'3" and 109 pounds, you don't have "standing," because the law in question doesn't affect you personally. Even dating a fat person isn't enough.

This explains why you often see six-year-old kids as the nominal plaintiffs in school desegregation cases, or senile derelicts as the nominal plaintiffs in welfare litigation. They've been recruited by lawyers. They don't know what the hell these people in suits are fighting about, but they have standing.

Jurisdiction

The concept of jurisdiction relates to which courts can hear which cases. You can't always get your case into a federal court, for example, even though that Oklahoma state judge won't read your papers and hates you because you have a beard, or don't have a beard, or anything else he feels like holding against you.

To understand jurisdiction, just recall how things worked when you were a kid: "cases" involving who got to use the family car probably fell within Dad's jurisdiction; those involving whose turn it was to do the dishes fell within Mom's. If it wasn't clear who had jurisdiction, you engaged in "forum shopping"—you went to the one most likely to give the answer you wanted.

The basic jurisdictional rule is that everything goes into the state courts unless there's a special reason it should go into a federal court. Lawyers would *rather* have their cases in federal court, partly because the judges are better and the rules of the game a lot clearer, but mainly because of prestige. A lawyer who says "I'm trying a case in *federal* court" is boasting. One who says "I'm trying a case in *state* court" is telling you where he's trying his case.

The reason for the prestige of federal cases is that they involve more money. The reason for the extra money goes back to the nature of jurisdiction.

There are two ways a federal court can get jurisdiction over a case. The first involves somebody going up against a federal law, *i.e.,* a law passed by the U.S. Congress (as opposed to one passed by a state, a city, or the Moral Majority).

A case involving a federal law usually involves a lot of money because Congress only passes laws on important subjects, like requiring those "Do Not Remove" labels on your pillows and mattresses that always make you tear the fabric to get them off. Congress leaves minor things like murder and rape to the states.

The second way a federal court can get jurisdiction over a case involves the state citizenship of the parties to the lawsuit. If the plaintiff (the fellow with the tire tracks on his face) is from Alabama, and the defendant (the fellow who was driving the cement truck) is from New York, the two parties have "diversity of citizenship." The case can get into federal court as a so-called "diversity suit." *

The theory behind this is that an Alabama jury might not take kindly to a New Yorker. The fact that *no one* takes kindly to a New Yorker is irrelevant. Supposedly the federal judge, appointed by the President, hates New Yorkers less than most people do, and he'll keep the Alabama jury from doing a bankroll-ectomy on the New Yorker.

Like cases involving federal laws, diversity suits tend to involve a lot of money—it costs more to run over somebody twelve states away than to run over your next-door neighbor. Hence the extra prestige of a federal case.

Service of Process

Long before you can begin to explain to a jury how you were sexually harassed by your lecherous boss, you have to give your boss notice

---

* Not to be confused with the plaid suit, striped shirt, and paisley tie that your Uncle Pollard from Kansas City wears to church.

of the lawsuit. She's entitled to defend herself.

You give her notice by delivering to her, or "serving" upon her, a copy of your complaint. This is called "service of process."

Service of process raises many practical questions. If you go to your boss's address and she won't open the door, how do you serve her? By placing it on her doorstep? Throwing it through her window? Beating her dog until she opens the door?

One option is to hire an independent agent to perform the service. A private process server, usually a former bar bouncer or mud wrestler, will lurk in the shadows of her home until he catches her, invariably scaring her into a coronary. (*See* Torts.)

The problem with private process servers is that they are not known for their reliability. The job doesn't pay well, and not that many people enjoy lurking in the shadows of strangers' homes.

Private process servers are famous for tossing complaints into the nearest sewer —"sewer service." Then they report back to you for payment. Because private

SURE-FIRE CLASS ACTIONS

Some of the best class actions are still waiting to be brought. Consider the following sure-fire winners:

1. A suit against Colgate-Palmolive on behalf of Ultra-Brite users who never scored.

2. A suit against NBC on behalf of television viewers who stayed up for the "Tonight Show" and got Joan Rivers.

3. A suit on behalf of purchasers of Raid who still have roaches the size of hamsters.

4. A suit on behalf of Wheaties eaters who couldn't take on their grandmothers.

5. A suit against Brooks Brothers on behalf of people who think paying top dollar for clothes entitles them to courteous service.

6. A suit on behalf of *Cosmopolitan* readers who still haven't achieved multiple ecstasy.

process servers outweigh you by 80 pounds, you pay without question.

Mr. T—potential private process server.

Class Actions

Contrary to what you might think, a "class" action is not an action between people who shop at Brooks Brothers and vacation at Saratoga. It is a lawsuit with lots of people on one side or the other.

Class actions are important to know about because they're incredibly lucrative for lawyers. Consider a suit you might bring against ABC on behalf of viewers of 20/20 who came down with lockjaw after prolonged exposure to Barbara Walters: you sue for $10 million, settle for $2 million, and keep $500,000 for your fee—all without even lifting a briefcase.

Class actions consistently involve a lot of money, as the people in a given class may number in the thousands, and they invariably settle before trial, because wealthy corporate defendants (carefully chosen by you after reviewing their balance sheets and income statements) know juries will stick it to them if given half a chance. Whenever a big class action settles, the lawyer goes home a wealthy individual.

The most famous class action involved a taxicab company in New York that had adjusted all its meters to charge illegally high rates, cheating thousands of people out of a few dollars each. Some lawyer filed a complaint on behalf of the "class" of cheated taxi passengers in Manhattan.

As this case made clear, class actions are not always simple affairs: how many people were cheated? Out of how much? Who were they? Don't all taxi drivers rip people off?

The bugs still haven't been worked out of class ac-

tion suits, but it's worth your while to stick with them. For plain old filthy lucre, a lawyer can't do better.

TORTS
(Ambulance Chasing for Fun and Profit)

If you plan to get wealthy as a litigator, you need to master torts along with civil procedure—civil procedure tells you *how* to sue someone, torts tells you *what* to sue him for.

The first issue you need to understand in the area of torts is: what *is* a tort?

If someone stabs you, there are three ways he could get into trouble. First the government could prosecute him. Stabbing someone is a crime. It has been for years.

Second, if you and your assailant had previously exchanged promises not to stab each other, you could sue him for breach of contract. He *promised* not to do it.

Third, you could sue him for carving you up. You could demand payment for your hospital bills, your pain and suffering, your prosthetic navel. What is the legal theory on which you could sue him? (You always need a theory.) He has committed a "tort"—in this case, the tort of redecorating your body without your consent.

A tort is anything you can sue someone for. Except breach of contract—that's called breach of contract.

So, if the *government* takes the case to court, it's a "crime" (in all instances that you need to worry about). If *you* take it to court, and there was no contract, it's a tort.

Once you've got a handle on what a tort is, all you have to do to bring a lawsuit is pick a tort, any tort. If you don't like the selection, feel free to make up your own (explaining it to the judge as a logical step in an already apparent trend in the law).

The One-Bite Rule

To get you going, consider a classic theme of tort law, the "one-bite rule."

The One-Bite Rule—make that first bite count.

Normally a dog owner may allow his dog to run freely through his neighborhood. This is not considered objectionable, because dogs are common domestic pets and usually don't bite people —unlike, say, elephants, which must be securely leashed.

What if your adorable Great Dane Gaylord rips a 40-stitch gash in your neighbor's right arm? Good old playful

Gaylord—*you* know he was just being affectionate. But your crabby neighbor, now called "Lefty," is upset. Can Lefty sue you and win?

No. You were not "negligent." You had no reason to think Gaylord would bite anyone. You did not fail to act like that famous figure of tort law, the "reasonable, prudent person."

Lefty's gash is just his bad luck—like a tornado, flood, or rhino stampede.

But what about rabid dogs? They're *known* to bite people. What about that German shepherd as big as a Volkswagen that moved into the neighborhood just about the time your cat disappeared?

More important, what about *Gaylord,* now that he has "known vicious propensities"?

For such animals, judges developed the "one-bite rule." After one bite, you're on notice that the animal is dangerous. For every bite thereafter you can be held liable.

The lesson from this is clear: don't squander that first free bite. Make it count.

False Imprisonment

Another classic tort, a darling of law professors, is "false imprisonment." Contrary to what you might think, this doesn't refer to the blunders of policemen who pounce on you, handcuff you, rough you up, and fingerprint you down at the station—all because they think you resemble Son of Sam. Not even if you look more like Truman Capote than Son of Sam.

False imprisonment is what you sue young thugs for when they surround your car and won't let you out. False imprisonment could also be what your neighbor sues you for when Gaylord chases him up a tree and won't let him down until you call Gaylord home for dinner. The key is impairment of someone's freedom of movement.

Law professors love to pose the question: What if someone locks your door for several hours while you're asleep so that you can't get out, but you don't *know* you can't get out. False imprisonment?

As an academic matter,

who knows? Who *cares?* As a practical matter, if you have a client to whom this has happened, go for it! The jurors will identify with the sleeping party and be incensed at the thought of someone hanging around outside the door. They'll think, "What if I woke up and had to go to the bathroom?"

Res Ipsa Loquitur

If you're going to get a jury to award you or your client money because of someone's tort, you of course have to convince them the tort actually happened. Usually you do this by eyewitness testimony: you get the bum who was asleep in a nearby alley to swear your client had a green light when the bus hit him.

But what if there were no eyewitnesses? What if the bum is so far gone that he can't get the story straight? All is not lost—you resort to the doctrine of *res ipsa loquitur*. This is Latin for "the thing *(res)* speaks *(loquitur)* for itself *(ipsa)*."

Note that the words are out of order. No wonder Latin is a dead language.

The actual case that gave rise to this doctrine involved a fellow who was walking along one day minding his own business, when out of the blue he was crushed over the head by a falling barrel of flour. He didn't see it coming. He didn't know where it came from. He just woke up in the hospital covered with flour and looking like the Pillsbury doughboy.

He sued the owner of the nearby building, insisting that the owner or one of his employees must have pushed the barrel out the window. The problem was that the victim couldn't prove it. He hadn't seen anything.

He prevailed anyway. The judge said that in some cases the negligence is so apparent from the circumstances that proof isn't necessary. He said, "The thing speaks for itself." The only question is, why did the judge say it in Latin?

Proximate Causation

A final subject you need to understand if you're going to line your wallet on the basis of someone's tort is the concept of "proximate causation."

Every event has millions of causes. Say your son Johnny is injured when he falls off the new bicycle you gave him for Christmas. Who or what *caused* his injury?

Did the bicycle company cause it by manufacturing a defective bike? Did the city cause it by failing to fill in those potholes that swallow buses whole? Did Gaylord cause it by leaping at Johnny with that "dinner time" look in his eyes? In theory, "causation" could be traced all the way back to Jesus of Nazareth for "causing" you to celebrate Christmas.

The judges who have addressed this subject say you have to identify the "proximate" cause of the event in order to assign liability. This doesn't resolve the problem, however. Of all the possible causes of your son's injury, only Jesus's birth can be excluded for not being a proximate cause—and plaintiffs' lawyers would concede this only because of the service-of-process problems involved.

The idea that each event has a "proximate" cause really doesn't help at all. It just gives judges a label to apply to whomever they want to stick with the cost of the accident. In this case, the judge would probably assign liability to the bicycle company. It has all the money. Who cares that the judge's wisdom and charity will make Johnny's younger brother's bike cost $10.00 more next Christmas?

REAL PROPERTY
(Dirt and Things Thereon)

Every lawyer should be familiar with the law of real property. For one thing, it's a jargon-filled area, requiring fluency in Latin and Olde English. When other lawyers try to intimidate you with terms like easement, seisin, and quitclaim, you need to know enough to be able to come right back at them with terms like caduceus, terpsichorean, and amanuensis. Besides, understanding real property law is the only way to keep that sleazy real estate agent from ripping you off on the purchase or sale of your house.

Real property covers two categories of things: (1)

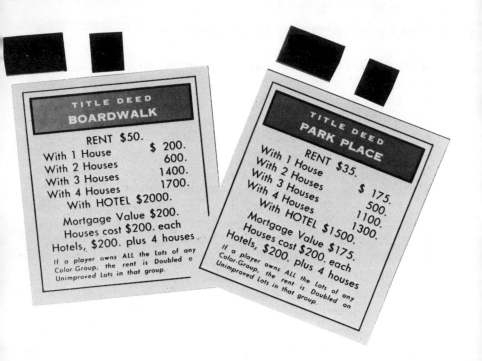

land, earth, soil, dirt—everything along these lines except what your potted plant is sitting in and what accumulates between your toes after you've been wearing sandals a while, and (2) "fixtures," *i.e.,* buildings and other items so large, heavy and immobile as to be virtually part of the land. This latter category includes Caucasian basketball players.

Real property law is a game of labels. For example, if someone sells you an acre of farm land, and it's yours, and you can do whatever you want with it, you don't just say it's *your land;* you say that you hold a "fee simple absolute" interest in that land.

Say you want to give a favorite plot of land to your brother and his kids. (You hate your own kids. They bear an uncanny resemblance to the local tennis pro, whom the guys around the club refer to as Tyler the Wonder Horse.) Moreover, you want to make sure that it stays in your brother's family as long as he has heirs.

In this case you don't just give your brother the deed with the restrictions scribbled on the back. You give him a "fee tail" interest in the land.

There are scores of these kinds of labels. They don't make sense. They don't sound like anything you've ever heard of. You just have to memorize them.

Consider the following rules that every law student must know by heart for his final exam in real property:

Of the defeasible estates, the fee simple determinable, a.k.a. fee simple on a special limitation, creates a possibility of reverter in the grantor and an executory interest in the third person, whereas the fee simple subject to a condition subsequent creates a power of termination, a.k.a. right of entry, in the grantor, as well as an executory interest in the third person. The

---

DEED

THIS DEED, made and entered into this 23rd day of May, 1626, by and between PETER MINUIT, Royal Governor of New Amsterdam, for and on behalf of the Empire of the Netherlands ("Purchaser"), and BUCOLIC BUFFALO, Chief, for and on behalf of the Carnarsee Native Americans ("Seller"):

WITNESSETH:

That for and in consideration of trinkets and low-grade cloth equal in value to no less than SIXTY (60) GUILDERS or TWENTY-FOUR (24) DOLLARS, receipt of all of which is hereby acknowledged, and the pipe of peace having been smoked, the Seller does hereby grant, bargain, sell and convey, with GENERAL WARRANTY of title, unto the Buyer, all that certain parcel of land situate in the New World and being more particularly described as follows:

An asphalt island, presently known as The Big Apple and also sometimes referred to as Manhattan or The City, located approximately in the North Atlantic Ocean and bounded by the Hudson, Harlem and East Rivers.

This conveyance is made subject to all liens, encumbrances and rights-of-way of record.

WITNESS the following signatures:

Peter Minuit

PETER MINUIT

X Bucolic Buffalo   *by Peter Minuit*

BUCOLIC BUFFALO

possibility of reverter is alienable, devisable, and descendable. In contrast, the power of termination is devisable and descendable but not capable of *inter vivos* transfer.

The astonishing thing about these rules is that every one of them is true!

Squatters' Rights

A peculiar but important concept of real property law is that you can acquire valid legal title to a piece of land simply by taking it and holding onto it for a long time. This method of acquiring land is known as "adverse possession."

It isn't quite as easy as it sounds. First, you really have to *have* the land. The courts say your use and possession of it must be "actual." If you decide you'd like three feet of your neighbor's lawn for a croquet field, it's not enough just to *proclaim* that the three feet are yours. You have to put up your wickets and start playing.

Second, your use must be "open" and "hostile." You can't just hop onto the lawn at night, wearing dark clothes and sneakers, and have a friend snap a flash photo of you to prove you were there. And you can't sucker your neighbor by telling him you're just borrowing the space for a while, like a cup of sugar. You have to be claiming it's *yours*. Guard dogs and spring guns would help satisfy this requirement.

Third, your use of the land has to be "exclusive." If three other neighbors are growing tomatoes on the turf you're trying to claim, you lose.

Fourth, you have to use the land "continuously." If you want it so badly, and you're too cheap to pay for it, cancel your world cruise. Scratch your tour of duty with the French Foreign Legion. You have to *be* there.

Finally, you have to hold the land and satisfy all these other requirements for *twenty years*. This is the hard part. This is what keeps you from pitching tent on your neighbor's lawn with the idea of fighting him off tooth and nail until title changes hands—this and the fact that if he calls the police they'll throw you in the slammer for trespass.

If you could fulfill all these requirements—it has happened twice in the last 400 years—your neighbor's lawn could be yours. You could leave him singing the adverse possession blues.

With this information and a lot of patience, you could take over North Dakota. How do you think the DuPonts got Delaware?

The Rule Against Perpetuities

The most irritating feature of real property law is the Rule Against Perpetuities. You know that great piece of farmland in Kentucky where your father grew up? Or that wonderful parcel of undisturbed beachfront turf in Big Sur where you've vacationed for years and that you want to make sure stays in the family forever? You can't do it. The Rule Against Perpetuities won't let you.

First announced in 1681 by the celebrated William of Nottingham, the Rule Against Perpetuities provides as follows:

> A contingent future interest which, by any possibility, may not vest within 21 years after some life in being when the interest is created, is void in its inception.

The main point, according to modern theologians, is that no one should be able to control a piece of land forever. William of Nottingham might have wanted his back-forty acres in England to remain farmland until the end of time, but his desires in 1681 should not control the use of the land today. Similarly Butch of Detroit might like the idea of his two acres on the South Side remaining a parking lot throughout eternity, but people in the year 2500 should have the right to dump nuclear waste there if it seems appropriate.

The Rule Against Perpetuities has inspired endless pages of discussion. These pages would have been more usefully employed on spools in Howard Johnson restrooms along I-95.

If you were studying the Rule Against Perpetuities in law school, your final exam would require you to apply it to a hypothetical such as the following:

> A to B for the life of C, remainder to D's heirs, so long as D has heirs, but if C's first born should be of another race,

then to E's heirs for so long as B's grand-children may reside in Cleveland, then to such heirs of B as may survive the then living residents of Staten Island.

You would have three minutes to answer this question.

LAW REVIEW

The heart of law school is course work. There's a lot of it (some of the casebooks come with wheels), and any-one who tells you otherwise is yanking your chain. Never-theless, there are other things around to use up your time. The one you hear the most about is the Law Review.

At every law school about 10 percent of the top students are invited to write on the school Law Review. Getting on the Law Review is the highest distinction a law student can acquire. If you make Law Review, according to popular myth, the world is your oyster. With that acco-lade you can get a job at the highest paying, hardest work-ing sweatshop in New York City.

Why is the Law Review considered so significant? Employers value the Law Re-view credential because noth-ing else offers so much tedious, petty gruntwork. Anyone who can put up with it has real potential for suc-cess in private practice.

What do people on the Law Review do? First you have to understand what a Law Review is, namely, a monthly magazine (actually, four to eight issues per year, depending on the school in question)* containing stu-dent and professional pieces whose merit is judged on their obscurity and their ratio of footnotes to text. (An ac-ceptable ratio is 5 to 1).

Law Review "staffers" or "members" (second-year students) write the student pieces, called "Notes" or "Comments." Staffers also "citecheck" each other's pieces and professional pieces.

---

* Curiously, there is rarely a corre-lation between the month designated on each issue and the month of actual pub-lication. When such a correlation occurs, there is a disparity between the *year* des-ignated and that of publication.

Law Review "editors" and members of the administrative board (the Editor-in-Chief, the Managing Editor, the Editor of Italics and Punctuation) run the operation. They review the professional pieces and presume to edit them.** They "instruct" the staffers with the self-confidence of grade school safety patrollers directing traffic.

If you have a chance to join your school's Law Review, you should take it. It *is* a handy credential. More important, the Law Review offices and library give you a place to hang your hat, as well as a nice place to study when college groupies have rendered the main law library unfit for work.

** The story is still told of the Articles Editor at Columbia who presumed to edit an article by the renowned British jurisprudential philosopher H.L.A. Hart. Professor Hart's characterizations of the editing ranged from "utterly ridiculous" to "incomprehensible." Only the intervention of sober authorities at Columbia saved the article for that school's Law Review.

**Citechecking
(Should this comma be
italicized?)**

Law reviewers spend most of their time not reading or writing but "citechecking" the things they publish. "Substantive" checking entails reviewing the sources you cite to make sure they actually say what you've said they say. "Technical" citechecking entails reviewing all

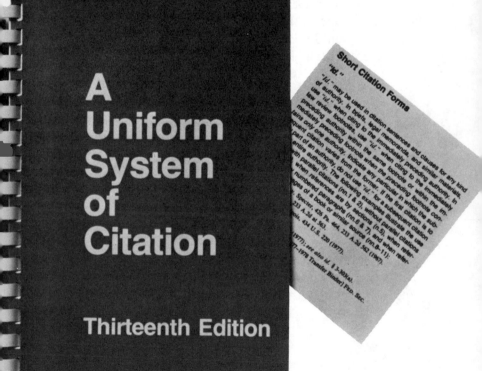

citations to confirm their propriety of *style*. The latter is by far the more important.

The universally recognized authority on legal style is a 237-page paperback volume entitled *A Uniform System of Citation,* commonly known as "the Blue Book" (from its color, which was once white, although people called it the Blue Book even then). The Blue Book tells you which words to abbreviate and how; which titles to italicize and when; what numbers to spell out and where. It tells you not to leave a space between initials in personal names: "W.C. Fields." Rule 6.1(a).

No wonder lawyers hold the Blue Book in awe, not unlike the way Moslems view the Koran.*

---

* The authors of the Blue Book consist of the top editors from three of the nation's leading Law Reviews, Columbia, Harvard, and the University of Pennsylvania, plus some from Yale. The current editors of these publications meet every four years to consider anew what inside jokes they can squeeze into the minutiae of the Blue Book. At present it is replete with obscure references to friends, enemies, lovers, and colorful professors of succeeding generations of law reviewers. *Compare* the names of the authorities cited in Rules 3.6 and 10.2.1(g) *with* the names on the masthead of the 1980 Columbia Law Review.

Blue Book Quiz

What really distinguishes a law reviewer from any other law student? His Blue Book expertise. He displays it proudly, a badge of honor, only too happy to instruct his inferiors on such questions as the citation of articles within articles collected in multivolume, multiple-edition, foreign-language treatises.

You don't have to take that crap. You, too, can acquire the necessary Blue Book mastery to make you a leader of the profession. But first you need to know where you presently stand. Test yourself with the following Quiz, which contains questions any self-respecting law reviewer could answer in his sleep. (Answers and a grading scale appear on p. 56.)

1. When citing the supplement to a state code, do you provide the date of the main volume?

2. How long must a passage be before you can quote it without quotation marks and indent it left and right?

3. For presidential proclamations, do you cite to

the Code of Federal Regulations (C.F.R.) or the Federal Register (Fed. Reg.)?

4. When citing case names in briefs and legal memoranda, *e.g., "Plum v. Rox,"* do you underscore the "v" along with the names of the parties?

5. When citing an unenacted federal bill, do you cite to the session of Congress in which it was passed, or to the page of the *Congressional Record?*

6. When citing multiple subsections within a single statutory section, do you use one or two section symbols (§§)?

7. For what books and pamphlets must you cite not only the date of publication but also the date of the first edition?

8. What is the only part of the United States Constitution which must be capitalized?

9. In quotations, do you use ellipses to indicate language deleted from the beginning of a sentence?

10. What is the only item of punctuation incapable of being italicized?

Quiz Answers

1. Not unless a portion of the statute being cited appears in the main volume. Rules 3.2(c), 12.3.1.

2. Fifty words. Rule 5.1(a).

3. The C.F.R., if possible. Otherwise, to the Fed. Reg. Rule 14.5.1.

4. Yes. Rule 1.1(b).

5. Always the former; also the latter, if possible. Rule 13.2.

6. One. Rule 3.4(b).

7. Those published before 1870. Rule 15.4(c).

8. The Bill of Rights. Rule 8.

9. Not if the quoted language can stand by itself as a full sentence. Rule 5.3(i).

10. The period. This isn't in the Blue Book, but law reviewers know it.

Evaluating Your Results

Correct Answers:

8–10	Advanced mastery; potential judge.
5–7	Respectable, but Wall Street partnership is doubtful.

2–4   Seriously   deficient;
lucky to hold position
with in-house counsel
of fertilizer company.

0–1   Not cut out for law;
better suited to profes-
sional boxing.

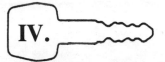

IV.

Summer Clerkships
(SUMMER CAMP FOR THE INCURABLY OVERACHIEVING)

Many students at the top law schools around the country spend the summer after their second year of law school "clerking" at a law firm. Summer clerkships are not unlike your high school prom, where you dressed like an adult, drank like an adult, and tried to fool around like an adult . . . and later learned it didn't come close to the real thing. Summer clerkships *resemble* actual private practice, but there are significant differences of which law students should be aware.

Socially, summer clerkships can be pleasant indeed. Most firms, particularly the large ones, wine and dine their summer clerks like visiting dignitaries. This routine contains elements of the comical and the fraudulent.

It is comical because of the disparity between the actual contribution of the clerks to the work of the firm and the attention accorded them; few summer clerks really pay their way, and *no* summer clerks really command the respect of the senior partners.

It is fraudulent simply because it is so unrealistic. To be sure, it happens every summer without fail. But the conviviality and gregariousness do *not* continue through the fall, winter and spring. It is a seasonal phenomenon, and its focus is narrow. A summer clerk would do well to ask himself why that senior partner who strolls through the library says hello to him but not to the full-time associates. Does the partner remember the associates' names? Did he know their

names when they were summer clerks? Did something change when they signed on permanently?

Professionally, as well as socially, summer clerkships depart from reality. A lot of firms engage in "cream skimming," *i.e.,* reserving for summer clerks all the interesting projects around the office (a big firm may have two or three in a summer). This is why so many summer clerks are later surprised to find that their positions as full-time associates offer all the dignity and job satisfaction of cleaning up Madison Square Garden after the International Horse Show.

More important, firms let slide a lot of mistakes committed by summer clerks that would cost a full-time asso-

ciate her job, or even her dictaphone. It is perfectly reasonable that firms should allow for youth and inexperience, but as a summer clerk you will rarely if ever be *told* of your shortcomings. Unless you screw up something serious—such as misspelling a partner's name in a memorandum—you will be told only that you did a fine job, made a lot of friends, and everyone is eager to have you back. If you do return to the firm, you will naturally return as well to the habits and techniques that you thought served you so well, only to discover—*after* the black marks are on your record—that those habits and techniques are about as acceptable as white socks.

TO SPLIT OR NOT TO SPLIT

More and more law students are splitting their summers, spending one half of the summer at one firm and the other half at another, usually in two remote places (say, Wall Street and midtown). The obvious benefit is that a student gets to check out two firms in a single summer, as well as romp across the country at someone else's expense.

Law firms don't like splits. They tolerate splits only because competition for the top students forces them to do so. A split prevents the firm from scrutinizing the clerk as closely as it would like. Also, at the end of a split, the clerk usually has two offers, rather than one, and he doesn't feel compelled to return to either of the two firms simply because it's more familiar and he can find the restroom without a map.

Should a clerk split? Absolutely. The differ- ence between what you'd learn about a firm in a full summer and what you can learn about it in half a summer doesn't begin to offset the informative value of looking at two different operations. The people who tell you otherwise are people who didn't split.

Some law firms will try to scare you out of splitting with stories of one clerk or another who screwed up early on and then, because he was splitting, didn't have time enough to redeem himself and salvage an offer.

In most instances a clerk who screwed up that badly couldn't have resurrected himself if he were the messiah. He couldn't have salvaged an offer with six more *months,* much less six more weeks. Such a clerk is plainly better off putting his mistake behind him and moving on to where he'll enjoy a clean slate.

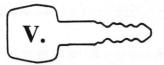

V

The Bar Exam

(THOUSANDS OF MORONS HAVE PASSED IT—SO CAN YOU)

The first thing you will encounter upon graduation from law school is the bar exam. A few slackers postpone it until after their judicial clerkships (*see* Chapter VI), and people who go straight into teaching indulge the hope of avoiding it forever. The wiser course is to bite the bullet and take it, if for no other reason than to be able to tell your parents you're finally equipped to get a job.

Passing the bar does not require extraordinary intelligence. If you doubt this, stroll down to the nearest courthouse and check out the first lawyer you meet.

Passing the bar does require one thing: a decent memory.

No matter how smart you are, you may not be able to figure out that the statute

Albert Einstein, Physicist—failed New York bar twice.

of limitations for indecent exposure in your state is three years, eight months and two days. No amount of intelligence can tell you the order of distribution of a limited partnerships' assets upon liquidation.

This brings us to the first of two rules for passing the bar: READ THE MATERIALS! The "materials" consist of two to four volumes that you can obtain from the bar review course in your state and that contain every point of law that might be covered on the exam.

Lots of these rules are arbitrary. You either know them or you don't. Intelligence doesn't come into play. Albert Einstein failed the New York bar twice.

You needn't memorize *all* these rules. Your goal is to pass, not to get the highest grade in the state.

Getting a high grade will be of absolutely no benefit. For one thing, no one will ever know. Not even you. You can't find out your score unless you fail.

How much effort is required? M.C.E. should be your guide. Minimum Critical Effort. The ideal grade is the lowest passing grade in the state.

You will hear stories of people who spent all summer at the beach,* glanced at the bar materials the night before, and then breezed through the exam. By and large these stories are in the same category as *Cinderella*. In any case, that approach is

---

*The bar exam is given in July and February across the nation. Most people take it in July following graduation, which means starting the two-month bar review course shortly after your last law school exam. This is hell.

too risky—you have to give it *something*.

What if you fail? Failing the bar is not the end of the world. It just feels that way.

Many bright people fail. Most go on to become judges and U.S. Congressmen.

Nevertheless, it is worth your while to try to pass it the first time around. February is a miserable time to be slogging across town for bar lectures, and your co-sufferers won't be wearing skimpy summer clothes with great tans.

This brings us to the actual taking of the exam, and to the second rule for passing: DO NOT PANIC!

There is no reason you *should* panic. You've taken hundreds of exams, and this one is different only in length (two days in most states; two-and-a-half in California, where everyone is too laid back to hurry).

People do get unusually nervous, however. The physical environment is unfamiliar. The people around you are strangers. The exam proctor couldn't find your name on his list.

If you feel a wave of panic about to come over you, try to nip it in the bud.

Remind yourself that you have never failed an exam in your life. If you have failed a number of exams in your life, remind yourself that no one has yet been jailed for failing the bar. (Usually you get a suspended sentence, with probation).

At the end of the second day, when the final "Put your pencils down" has been called, you will feel giddy, like a marathoner crossing the finish line. This is partly because of the nervous energy you have expended. It may also be because you have forgotten to eat for several days.

The best thing to do at this point is go home and take a nap. Fatigue contributes to depression.

Above all, do not talk about it! If you need to be told this after years of exams in college and law school, you are probably an incorrigible jerk. If that is the case, view this as a last chance to redeem yourself.

You will not get the results of the exam for three or four months. Without question, this waiting game is miserable.

The important thing to remember is that eventually you will pass. If not the first time, the second. Or the third. Everyone does.

What you should worry about is what comes after.

COPING WITH FEAR: CONTINUE TO WRITE!

You don't have to be a naturally timid person to experience fear during the bar exam. You could easily pick it up from somebody else.

Fear is contagious. When the person next to you begins to toss his cookies, you may begin to feel uncomfortable. This is understandable, like the feeling you get when the pilot of your airplane straps on his parachute.

Suppress this feeling. Continue to write. Whatever happens, continue to write.

If the person next to you has a heart attack, continue to write.

If *you* have a heart attack, try to gut it out until the proctor calls "Time!" If you can't last that long, be sure to gasp loudly or wave your arms to catch the proctor's attention; those around you with any sense will continue to write.

PANTHEON OF LEGAL GREATS
(AND NOT-SO-GREATS)

Every field of endeavor has its giants, and the law is no different. Consider the following titans, whose positions of prominence in the annals of American lawyerdom will always remain secure:

Clarence Darrow—*defense lawyer. More famous for the case he lost, the 1925 Scopes "monkey trial," than any he won. Immortal portrayal by Henry Fonda in* Inherit the Wind.

Louis D. Brandeis—*famous not only as a brilliant jurist and the first Jewish Supreme Court Justice, but also as the originator of "Brandeis briefs," mammoth sociological volumes that gave new meaning to "the weight of authority."*

William Howard Taft—*27th President of the United States, 10th Chief Justice of the Supreme Court. Too enthralled by the law even to take time off for exercise.*

FAMOUS PEOPLE YOU WOULD NEVER HAVE GUESSED WENT TO LAW SCHOOL

The universe of lawyers boasts not only a dazzling roster of persons famous for their contributions to the law, but also a colorful cast of characters distinguished in other ways:

Howard Cosell—*toupée model, sportscaster.*

Leo Tolstoy—*gentleman farmer, author.*

Archibald MacLeish—*bohemian, poet.*

Mahatma Gandhi—*weaver, politician.*

Warren Burger—*Chief Justice of Supreme Court.*

VI

Judicial Clerkships

(WHY WAIT UNTIL YOU'RE 50 TO PLAY GOD?)

Top law students spend time after graduation working as assistants to judges. These positions are called "judicial clerkships."

The label is unfortunate. When you tell laymen you're "clerking," they say, "Don't worry. I'm sure you'll be able to get a job with a private firm sooner or later." Laymen don't understand. The big advantage of clerking is that it enables you to begin work with a private firm later, rather than sooner.

Whether clerking is a great deal or merely a good deal depends on three things: the type of court, the judge, and the location.

Courthouse on the Island of Tobago. The Ultimate Clerkship.

The Location

Starting with the last first, the location is important for the obvious reason that it's more fun to spend a year in San Francisco or New York than Utah or Alaska—unless you're a Mormon or a walrus, and maybe even then.

The Judge

As for the judge, if he's brilliant, his clerks may learn something. If he's as thick as a giant redwood, the educational value of the experience may be less.

Even more important than the judge's intellect, however, is his work routine. Judges don't *need* to be workaholics; most aren't. They don't *have* to do anything that strikes them as unappealing; few do. But some judges seem to take their duties very seriously. They come into the office at dawn. They stay past dinner. They're in every Saturday. They drive their clerks crazy.

These judges should be avoided. At that pace you might as well work at a private firm and get paid for it.

The Court

There are two questions a prospective clerk should ask about the type of court:

(a) Is it a state court or federal court?

The best thing that can be said about clerking for a state court judge is that it beats unemployment—depending on the welfare allowances where you live. Not since Oliver Wendell Holmes left the Massachusetts Supreme Court has there been a state court judge whose name on your resumé would be of as much interest to prospective employers as where you went to summer camp.

The federal courts are a different story—except for the Tax Court, the Court of Claims, and a few others that no one is quite sure what they do.

A federal clerkship at any level offers decent pay, plenty of prestige, and considerable educational value. Unless the federal judge is stupid, mean, and located in

WHAT DO JUDICIAL CLERKS DO?

All judicial clerks do the same thing, namely, whatever their judges tell them to do. A few judges make their clerks pick up their laundry, help them on with their robes, or even perform menial chores. Generally, however, clerks do three things.

First, they deal with the mountains of paper that come in. Those $50,000 briefs that large law firms consider suitable for framing—clerks use them to soak up spilled coffee.

Second, clerks research the cases cited in the papers to make sure the lawyers aren't stretching the truth.*

---

* Actually, the substantive role of clerks is broader than that. They *explain* things to their judges, particularly in complex areas such as antitrust. *See The New York Times,* D-2 (March 8, 1983):

"Where do judges get their economics?" said Philip Areeda, a Harvard Law School antitrust professor. "From their law clerks."

This is a critical function, for obvious reasons.

Third, clerks write the final rulings, or "opinions," that go out under the judge's signature. There is debate in legal circles over how much opinion writing a judge should delegate to his clerks. Opinions are important things. They not only decide individual cases, from who gets the kids to whether *Penthouse* has defamed Miss Wyoming, but also set "precedents," which lawyers and clients theoretically look to in deciding whether to hire more minorities or tell the truth about the sawdust content of dogfood.

Good or bad, clerks have always pulled the main oar on opinion writing. In the final analysis, it's probably a good thing: clerks get to be clerks because they're bright; judges get to be judges because they know somebody.

Buffalo, you can't go too far wrong.

(b) Is it a high court or a low court?

There are three tiers in the federal court system: District Court (trial level), Circuit Court (intermediate level), and Supreme Court (top banana level).

The Supreme Court

Clerking on the Supreme Court is *the* legal credential, guaranteeing a faculty position at any school, or a drone position with any firm. More-over, it's fun. The clerks enjoy plush marble chambers, state-of-the-art word processing equipment, and a basketball court on the top floor—the highest court in the land.

Many of the clerks complain of the workload (particularly Justice Stevens's clerks, because there are only two, and Justice Blackmun's clerks, because there are only four), but this is like rich people complaining of difficulties in servicing their yachts. No sober person turns down a clerkship with "the Supremes."

The District Court

The District Court level is great, too. At this level the clerks see trials, confessions, and sentencings—which they savor with the bloodlust of plebeians at the Roman coliseum.

Moreover, they deal with attorneys on a daily basis. Litigators who wouldn't return a call to the President will come running out of the bathroom to catch a call from a clerk. The same partners who will be abusing the clerks when they become associates the following year now grovel before them without shame.

The Circuit Court

Of the three federal courts, the Circuit Court has the least going for it as a place to clerk. Its chief benefit is that it offers a better shot at a clerkship with the Supremes the next year than the District Court does.

The only contact a Circuit Court Clerk has with the outside world comes once a month when three-judge panels listen to oral arguments, with one lawyer saying the District Judge made a mistake, and the other lawyer saying he didn't.

They don't hear witnesses testify as to how the fight broke out; they don't see the tears of the spurned lover on the stand; they don't hear the convicted defendant screaming "Prison bars can never hold me" as he is dragged away. Clerking on the Circuit Court is as much like the Law Review as a job could be.

VII.

Recruiting
("A DIAMOND AS BIG AS THE RITZ")

Recruiting has much in common with fraternity rush: both involve forced smiles, frequent handshakes, too much to drink, questions that no one cares about the answers to, and a general lack of dignity.

Recruiting is important, however. Let's face it: getting a job is what it's all about. No one goes to law school because he can't think of anything else to do with all his money and free time.

There are as many sizes and kinds of law firms as you can imagine. Firms range in size from several hundred in a single city (Shearman & Sterling, with over 350 lawyers in New York), to several hundred in lots of cities (Baker & McKenzie—"the McDonalds of law firms"— with over 620 lawyers around the world), to the solo practi-

tioner (Larry "Was-that-a-siren?" Durkin, with a part-time secretary in Lubbock).

Some firms specialize in a single area of the law, such as communications (usually in Washington, D.C.), energy (usually in Houston), or extortion (usually in Arizona).

Regardless of what kind of firm you want to work for, you need to know how to handle yourself on the recruiting circuit.

The primary rule to keep in mind about recruiting is that law firms, like lemmings, have no independent sense of judgment. They want you if they think their competitors want you. They're less interested in your credentials than in how their competitors view your credentials. Thus, your basic goal is to make them think other leading firms have already made you an offer or

75

"Nice guys, but an odd firm . . . they practice the law of the jungle."

are on the verge of doing so.

This doesn't mean you have to lie to anyone. You can achieve the desired effect simply by dropping the names of the leading firms in town—what you've heard about them, how they seemed when you interviewed with them, why you're not sure which one is best for you. For example:

• "I understand Sullivan & Cromwell is frequently confused with Solomon & Cohen—has this firm encountered similar problems?"

If anyone asks if these firms have actually made you an offer, you can usually say that you haven't heard from them yet—which is particularly true if you've never interviewed with them.

(A) INTERVIEWING

In order to get a job at a law firm, you have to survive two stages of interviews: the on-campus screening and the full-scale assault at the firm's offices. Each of these stages calls for different strategies and techniques.

The On-Campus Interview

The on-campus interview lasts 20 to 30 minutes. If your resumé shows you're at the bottom of your class, there's nothing you can do in that brief a period to get a "call-back" to a leading firm, short of bribing the interviewer with a $2,000 hit of the leading export commodity of Bogotá. Conversely, if your resumé shows you to be a real star, you'll be hard put to *avoid* getting a call-back, unless you show up in a sweaty T-shirt and a Mr. T. haircut.

Most applicants fall somewhere between these extremes. If you're a member of this bland majority, it is essential that you master the fine points of the on-campus interview.

The on-campus interview is too short for you to figure out what substantive qualities the interviewer thinks are important and then persuade him you're chock full of these qualities. You have to score your big points in terms of personal style.

This means more than wearing matching socks, having your fly zipped, and remembering the name of the firm in which you're supposedly eager to spend the rest of your professional career.

It means being distinctive, memorable. It means not boring the crap out of the interviewer with loser questions you should already know the answer to ("How big is your firm?") or questions he's sure to have already heard 50 times ("Does your firm have a rotation system for new associates?") It means asking him questions about himself, rather than his firm, so he'll have an opening to talk about the subject in which he's most interested. (The applicant who does this is consistently remembered as a "delightful conversationalist.")

Prep yourself on the firm in advance (your law school library will have all sorts of data on file) so you can dazzle the interviewer with the inci- siveness of your questions. If you can find out in advance who the interviewer will be, prep yourself on *him* (the background of every lawyer

Interviews are no time to be shy. Law firms appreciate aggressiveness in their associates.

at every firm is in your library's *Martindale-Hubbell*), and drop complimentary remarks on his college, his military division, the year he was born.

Be diplomatic with this "informed" approach: the interviewer won't enjoy talking about the recent SEC censure of his senior partner, nor will he care to speculate on his brother's chances of parole. Within limits, however, familiarity with the firm and with him is a good thing.

Finally, if you have any choice in the matter, schedule yourself for the first interview in the morning (when the interviewer is still fresh) or the last interview of the afternoon (when he'll love you for being the last person he'll have to see). If you can't avoid a slot in the middle of the day, be ready to come on strong with the references to other top firms.

The Office Call-Back

The most important thing to remember about the office call-back is to go easy on the coffee and tea. Every person you meet will offer you some, and you cannot win the "battle of the bladder."

Otherwise your strategy should be pure Dale Carnegie: talk about whatever your interviewers find most interesting. For lawyers, again, this means talking about themselves.

It isn't hard to get them going. Ask them what kind of law they practice, how long they've been at it, what got them into it. Lawyers love contemplating their origins and destinies.

Toward the end of an interview with a partner, throw in a question or two about the firm and its practice, just to let him know you're a serious worker. You'll strike a particularly responsive chord if you inject references to "billings" and "profits"—anything related to money.

With an associate, you're as well off not asking about the firm at all. The associate has probably just turned away from ten or twelve legal documents with pages numbering in the triple figures, and the last thing he

If all else fails, what's a little begging when your career is at stake?

wants to talk about in this hiatus is more law.

At some point in your interview with an associate, express your concern as to whether partners are able to appreciate the talents of their associates. Every associate feels unappreciated, and this comment will render you instantly likeable in his eyes. Don't make it obvious that you're cultivating him and that you don't really care about his views on the firm; tell him you already have the hard data, and now you're just trying to get a feel for the place. Then let him go on as long as he likes.

If you ever find yourself short on conversation topics, take note of the trappings of your interviewer's office. The things he has on display are things he *likes* to talk about. If he has an oar hanging on his wall, ask him if by chance he once rowed crew. If he has a picture of himself and a former president on the wall, ask him how he got to know Dick or Jerry or Jimmy. You're probably best off *not* attempting to compliment an old geezer on the lovely picture of his granddaughter—it could turn out to be his latest wife.

The Recruiting Lunch

A standard part of the recruiting ritual is an expensive lunch. When you're an indigent student, this can be a major occasion, both as the first square meal you've had in weeks and as your first taste of legal largesse.

If you're in the right frame of mind, a recruiting lunch can be a lot of fun. The escorts will usually be associates, rather than partners, and the associates will take full advantage of the outing to enjoy themselves and run up an enormous bill they can charge to the firm.

A recruiting lunch can also be a prime opportunity to get the real scoop on the firm, depending on how many drinks the associates have and whether they're the sort who feed on one another's gripes: "You think *you* got shafted by that partner; listen to what the son of a bitch did to *me* two days ago. . . ." Encourage them to continue in this vein.

You should feel free to join your hosts in their indulgence in wine, brandy, chocolate mousse, or whatever. This is part of your reward for accumulating a good record. Besides, if they're clearly out for a good time, you don't want to spoil it.

Above all, do not feel guilty about the cost of the meal. It's not *your* fault they're trying so hard to impress you. Besides, the firm will take it out of you or some other associate later on.

THE RESUMÉ

There's no point in producing a flashy resumé to assist you in finding a job with a law firm. Lawyers aren't businessmen; they don't know anything about packaging or merchandising and can't appreciate a good job of it on a resumé.

They're interested mainly in your grades in college and law school, and they *might* consider outside activities that show an unusual ability to stomach huge piles of grunt work. This does *not* include being a Red Cross donor or a bag boy at the local Hero Supermarket. It *does* include being a proofreader at the Sanskrit Publishing Center or shovelling horse manure at a fertilizer plant—*these* reflect on your ability to practice law.

If your grades are good, put them up front and center. That's easy. The big question is: what if your grades are terrible? What if the only "A" you ever got was in one of those touchy-feely, get-your-head-together social relations seminars in which everyone got A's because the bearded professor from California didn't like to pass "value judgments"?

It's a tough problem. Interviewers aren't just passing time when they inquire about your grades. The fact is that if your grades are really terrible, your first job, if you get a legal job at all, will probably be with the general counsel's office of the Metropolitan Toledo Sewer Authority (Field Division).

* * *

NOTE: regardless of your grades, don't clog up the personal section of your resumé by saying "Health: Excellent." Law firms don't care about your health. Check out the people who interview you, with their paunches, skinny arms and pale complexions: is *their* health excellent?

RECRUITING LUNCH DISASTERS

As relaxed as a recruiting lunch may seem, don't let down your guard. You're constantly on trial. Avoid any form of gaucherie, no matter how many rounds of applause it may have drawn in your fraternity or sorority dining room, and be particularly careful to avoid the following fatal blunders:

• At a Chinese restaurant, don't blow your nose or clean your glasses with the bread pancake that comes with the moo shu pork.

• At an Italian restaurant, never order spaghetti with meat sauce or anything else likely to get friendly with the front of your shirt.

• Wherever you are, don't touch the hard rolls; they always fall apart and generate a pile of crumbs as big as a basketball.

• Be reluctant to pop one of those round, pastry-like little balls into your mouth, because it is probably a ball of butter. If you make this mistake, do not attempt to ameliorate the situation by declaring, "Now *that's* a good butterball."

• If the bill passes within your visual range, do not let out a long low whistle and exclaim "Hot *damn,* they must think one of us broke a window!"

• If a little dish of water arrives at the end of the meal, don't drink it.

Recruiting Letters

Every recruiting letter has one of three basic messages: (1) yes; (2) maybe; (3) no. If the letter you get says "no," you don't care what else it might say. But if it says "maybe" or "yes," it's important for you to be able to read between the lines in order to know where you really stand. To aid you in this process, set forth on the following pages are two pairs of recruiting letters. In each pair, one letter shows you what the firm said, the other what the firm really meant.

THE "YES" LETTER   What the firm *said:*

Queen & Sprawling
1 Peachtree Street
Atlanta, Georgia 30319

November 23, 1983

Mr. James T. Pinch
906 Johnson Hall
Columbia Law School
New York, New York 11743

Dear Mr. Pinch:

I enjoyed talking with you when I was at Columbia. You have an excellent record, and on behalf of the firm I would like to extend you an offer of employment.

We would be pleased to have you visit our offices to meet more of our attorneys. If you would be interested in pursuing this invitation, please call me or our recruitment coordinator Ellen Shady to arrange a mutually convenient time for your visit.

I look forward to hearing from you soon.

Sincerely,

Barbara J. Bookman

What the firm *meant:*

Queen & Sprawling
1 Peachtree Street
Atlanta, Georgia 30319

November 23, 1983

Mr. James T. Pinch
906 Johnson Hall
Columbia Law School
New York, New York 11743

Dear Mr. Pinch:

For a guy from a trade school in Harlem, you make quite an impression. Your pale complexion and emaciated physique, combined with your incredibly high grade point average, suggest that you are precisely the sort of compulsive, library-loving grind we're looking for.

No doubt you will have a lot of offers, because hard-core zealots like you aren't a dime-a-dozen. Someone so patently willing to sacrifice his health and social life is a real find.

I wouldn't want to introduce you to a client or have to eat a meal with you, but I'll bet you could rack up enough billable hours in a year to reduce your salary to the equivalent of $1.95 per hour.

I hope we can sign you up.

Sincerely,

Barbara J. Bookman

Barbara J. Bookman

THE "MAYBE" LETTER   What the firm *said:*

CRAVEN, SWINE & LESS
43 Park Avenue
New York, New York 30319

November 23, 1983

Mr. Russell A. Williams
413 Johnson Hall
Columbia Law School
New York, New York 11743

Dear Mr. Williams:

I enjoyed talking with you when I was at Columbia. You have an excellent record, and although I am not able to make you an offer of employment based on our meeting, I would like very much to have you visit our offices for further interviews.

If you would be interested in pursuing this invitation, please call our recruitment coordinator Laurie Munch to arrange a mutually convenient time for your visit.

I look forward to seeing you again.

Sincerely,

G. Carter Covington

What the firm *meant:*

CRAVEN, SWINE & LESS
43 Park Avenue
New York, New York 30319

November 23, 1983

Mr. Russell A. Williams
413 Johnson Hall
Columbia Law School
New York, New York 11743

Dear Mr. Williams:

I must say I was surprised that a person like you would bother to interview with Craven, Swine & Less. Your record gives new meaning to the word mediocre.

On the other hand, a bald willingness to ask for something you have no right to is worth something in this line of work, as you'd understand if you could have heard some of the arguments we used recently in a big antitrust suit. You've definitely got guts.

You couldn't possibly have a real future with us. We always need more bodies, however, and you might be okay for two or three years. Besides, we can bill your time as highly as that of our good associates.

I'm not willing to take sole responsibility for hiring you, so you'd better come down and meet some others. Since you're in the same city it won't cost us much to have you in.

Sincerely,

G. Carter Covington

(B) RECRUITING MISREPRESENTATIONS

Law firm recruiters, like used car dealers, are known for their willingness to misrepresent reality. Their misrepresentations often deviate so far from reality as to constitute what laymen might call "lies."

The mere presence of a law firm recruiter has been known to cause a polygraph to blow a fuse.

"WE KEEP OUR ASSOCIATES INFORMED . . ."

December 15, 1983

MEMORANDUM

To: All Associates
From: The Administrative Committee
Re: Partners Meeting

At the Partners' Meeting of December 15, discussions were held on matters of mutual interest.

S.O.B.

The source of this tendency to falsehood in recruiters is not hard to find: in choosing their recruiters, law firms actively seek out those attorneys least burdened by a proclivity for truth. Some California firms sponsor contests to see who can tell the biggest whopper.

Lies told by recruiters and used car dealers are not punishable under the law. They're not even called "lies;" they're called "puffing." Examples of puffing by used car salesmen are: "There will always be a resale market for this Edsel," and "This Pinto couldn't be safer."

On the interviewing circuit you will encounter certain lies over and over again. Set forth below are ten of the most common recruiting lies, accompanied by a translation of what these lies really mean.

(C) "HARD QUESTIONS"

Interviews are no time for you to be a jellyfish. Go into every interview prepared

What Recruiters Say	**What Recruiters Mean**
1. Our associates work hard but like it.	1. Our associates work hard.
2. You'll get excellent training at this firm.	2. After three years here you'll have all the skills of a legal secretary.
3. We have one of the more diversified practices in the city.	3. We'll chase ambulances to get clients if we have to.
4. We believe in lean staffing of cases.	4. We make each associate do the work of three.
5. We don't spend the entire day at the office.	5. We take a lot of work home.
6. Our lawyers maintain a variety of outside interests.	6. Three years ago we had an associate whose wife used to play the piano.
7. This firm likes to keep a low profile.	7. No one has ever heard of this firm.
8. We encourage *pro bono* work.	8. We tolerate *pro bono* work on weekends.
9. We believe in bringing associates along one step at a time.	9. You'll be indexing deposition transcripts for years.
10. We have a policy of carefully controlled growth.	10. We're losing clients.

to ask the following ten sets of Hard Questions:

1. How does the firm determine associate salaries? Are raises and bonuses based on sheer merit, or instead on "productivity" (euphemism for "hours")? If productivity, does the calculation include *pro bono* work, client development, recruiting and other activities an associate may be "asked" to do but often gets no credit for?

2. What is the rate of associate turnover? How many have left in the past six months? The past two years?

3. What does the firm

"Then it's agreed. There is no place here for someone who marches to the beat of a different drummer."

offer in the way of associate training? Is it all "on the job" (*i.e.*, nothing)?

4. Are any associates working exclusively on a single big case? If so, will *I* be assigned to that sinkhole of a case?

5. Ask the associates who take you to lunch if they're on a special recruiting committee. How many lawyers in the firm don't see any recruits? (Lots of firms put their six or seven presentable people up front.)

6. How much *pro bono* work does the firm do, *as a percentage of its total billable work?* (Five percent is

UNDERSTANDING BILLABLE HOURS

When lawyers talk about billable hours, they usually refer to annual figures. Set forth below is a chart that breaks down the annual figures into weekly figures, and then puts them into perspective. In evaluating these figures, keep in mind that billable hours *should* not include time you spend eating lunch, calling all over town to get a date, or debating whether Ty Cobb was more important to baseball than Ted Williams. An accepted rule of thumb is that 40 billable hours requires 60 hours at the office.

Annual Total	Weekly Average (50 weeks)	Interpretation
4,000	80	Wrong profession; medical intern.
3,500	70	Pathological liar.
3,000	60	Barely conceivable, and then only if living with cot in office.
2,500	50	Sweatshop hours. Brutal, but conceivable, given lots of travel. Probably guilty of substantial bill padding.
2,000	40	Very respectable figure in most cities; requires regular weekend and evening work. Part-time in New York.
1,500	30	Civilized lifestyle, assuming no heavy non-billable duties. Total figure for 20-person firm in Los Angeles.
1,000	20	An associate with this number had better be working for his father's firm.
500	10	Partner.
0	0	Of Counsel.

THE OPEN-DOOR POLICY
"We welcome constructive criticism from our associates . . ."

Law firms boast of their openness to criticism and reform. They claim to observe an "open-door" policy with respect to associate grievances and speak of their eagerness for thoughtful suggestions from below.

Once you become an associate, try them out. Suggest keeping the office heat on during winter weekends because it's difficult for the associates to write while wearing ski mittens. Request facial quality toilet tissue in the associate restrooms.

The response from any partner you approach will consist of: "I'm glad you mentioned that. You know, it was a problem when I was an associate. It's a problem, sure enough."

This response is intended to convey the message, "I know how you feel. I've been there. I'm a regular guy."

It also says, "I'm not going to do anything about it. No one is. Take it like a man."

---

probably as much as you can expect.)

7. Did most of the partners go to the same school? Do most of them attend the same church, temple, shrine, or sacrificial altar?

8. How many hours does the firm's average associate bill each year? (This figure should be lower than the total number of hours in a year.) Does the firm announce a "budgeted" (euphemism for "required") number of billables? Is the budgeted number a *minimum,* or an *average?* What

So much for the open door policy.

Until you make partner, hang on to your ski mittens and a spare roll of Charmin.

ASSOCIATE COMMITTEES

If associates have grievances, why not unionize? Why not at least band together to make their views known, as through the formation of an associates' committee?

The basic reason is ambition—associates see no long-term benefit in improving the lot of associates, because they don't plan to *be* associates ten years down the road. They plan to become part of management.

Moreover, they know partners would view associate organization with the same cool, aw-they're - just - blowing - off - steam attitude with which George III viewed the Boston Tea Party. They know partners would be as enthusiastic about an associates' committee as Frank Perdue would be about a committee of oven-stuffer roasters.

were the billables of the last group of associates to make partner?

9. Does the firm have any "non-equity" partners, *i.e.*, people who are held out to the world as partners but in fact get a fixed salary, and are *not* tenured. ("Non-eq-uity" partnership is a sham device for postponing the day of *real* partnership, perhaps indefinitely.)

10. Ask an associate interviewer how he would characterize associate morale? How many headhunters have his resumé on file?

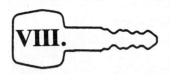

VIII

How to Survive (and Make Partner) in Your Law Firm

(YOU CAN MAKE IT TO THE TOP . . . IF YOU KNOW WHAT TO KISS, AND WHOSE)

Each day of associateship in a law firm is like walking a tightrope over shark-infested waters: one wrong step could spell doom. Most associates walk this tightrope with their eyes wide shut.

Survival is the name of the game, and in order to survive in a law firm, it is critical to keep in mind this simple fact: the partners run the show.

To be sure, some of them run more of it than others, and the idea (which they hold out to the public) that one is accepted as an equal upon attaining the status of "partner" is as accurate as saying Liechtenstein is the equal of Russia, because they're both "sovereign jurisdictions."*

Regardless, however, of any inequalities that may exist among the partners, they're tenured, and you're not. It is hard to get rid of one of them and easy to get rid of you. Therefore, your goal must be the cultivation of their approval.

Over time, this cultivation may become odious. As one associate commented, "They should make my senior partner Pope; that way all I'd have to kiss is his ring."

---

* Or that a '65 Impala is the equivalent of a Sherman tank because they get the same gas mileage.

"Remember Cogswell, associates are fungible, partners are not."

Assuming that you can stomach the thought of prolonged obsequiousness, how can you ensure that the partners will vote thumbs-up when your name comes up for partnership seven or eight years down the road?

There are two reasons any partner might vote to invite you into the partnership: (1) he likes you, or (2) he thinks you'll make him rich.

Practically speaking, he may like you *because* he thinks you'll make him rich—a not uncommon confluence of motivations. Just recall that great, warm-nosed dog you had as a child, which nuzzled up to you and wagged its tail when it saw you coming—as long as you continued to feed it.

Try to think of the partners as furry Labradors with unusually strong appetites.

In order to make the partners like you, you need to make them think you're *like* them, that you're one of them. You even want them to think of you as a surrogate son or daughter, unlike their actual sons and daughters, who wear long hair, snort cocaine, and aspire to play lead guitar with Sid Vicious and the Sex Pistols. Also, in order to make the partners think you'll make them rich, you need to convince them you're the hardest-working, least likely-to-screw-up, most anal, Puritanical grind since Cotton Mather.

To succeed in this dual quest, there are a number of specific rules that *must* be followed. These are key maxims that you would be well advised to tape to your bathroom mirror for review every morning as you tie your tie or trim your nose hairs.

Strict adherence to these rules could gain you a window office, with a secretary who will type one-page letters and deliver phone messages within several days of when they come in. Deviation from them could land you in an interior office across from the messengers' washroom, with a gay secretary who sends out your letters streaked with avocados and quiche.

RULE NO.1. COVER YOUR ASS (C.Y.A.)

This rule is the most important of all the rules, as well as the most difficult to adhere to. The reason it is difficult to adhere to is that its command embraces everything you do, no matter how trivial. A discussion of all the applications of this rule could fill several volumes, but for present purposes some examples will have to suffice:

• Supervise everything your secretary sends out in the mail. The stories are legendary of the wrong letter going out in the right envelope, or vice versa. If your secretary mixes up the memo you intended for your client, in which you observe that his gold bullion sales in Switzerland "might" have consequences for his income tax obligations, with the letter you intended for the Internal Revenue Service, saying your client has nothing else to report, you might as well start cleaning out your desk.
• Proofread everything —carefully. This is all the

more true when a partner hands you a document and says, "Take a quick look at this and then send it out. I'm sure it's fine." He might very well think it's fine when he gives it to you, but . . . why is he giving it to you?

What you're seeing is an instinctive effort to cover *his* ass. If a legal argument proves to have been stated inaccurately, or the numbers just don't add up, you can be certain that the next document you proofread will be your resumé. Remember: the last name on any brief, or the junior-most person associated with any project, is deemed responsible for the screw-ups of everyone.

"Bravo to you, sir, for those amazingly astute comments on the margins of my memo."

• Before sending out any brief, report, or other document, clear it first with anyone senior to yourself. For this purpose, a senior associate will do. The point is to place the responsibility for screw-ups anywhere but on yourself. Not only should you run any document past a senior person, but (a) dictate a "memo to file" that you've done so, and (b) somehow let an *even more senior* person know that you've cleared the document with the semi-senior person.

• Notify and consult the client regarding everything you do on his case or project. Clients don't affect you directly, but they can always complain to the partners, and in rare instances they will even get hot enough about something to sue the firm. Your aim should be to build a record—consisting of letters to the client covering *everything*—to put the client in the position of appearing responsible for anything that may screw up (which can happen for reasons totally beyond your control).

Partners, you will find, are the ultimate ass coverers in this fashion, spending

PUT THE BURDEN ON THE CLIENT

When writing a client to request that he sign an affidavit or "verify" a pleading, do not be too proud to include a weasely (yet legal sounding) line like the following:

"Please read, review, examine and consider all aspects of this item carefully, thoroughly and thoughtfully. Needless to say, you should feel perfectly, totally and absolutely free to make any additions, alterations, modifications, corrections, amendments, clarifications, enhancements, augmentations, editions or changes that you feel are appropriate, necessary, desirable, suitable, reasonable, worthwhile, or good. Thereafter, and only thereafter, if it meets with your full and complete satisfaction, agreement, approval and liking, sign it and . . ."

When you include this sort of line, the *client* is responsible for whatever you've produced, and your ass is covered. (For God's sake, keep a copy of your correspondence.)

enormous amounts of billable time drafting letters explaining to the client why the firm is doing what it is doing. This could all be done by telephone for one-tenth of the expense, but such a commonsense approach would reduce billings and—even more unacceptable—leave the firm's collective ass uncovered.

• In reporting meetings or conferences on your time sheets, never just say "Attended meeting with general counsel of client—2 hours." If a partner was there, he may have recorded the meeting on his time sheets as lasting only 1½ hours. Even if you were the only lawyer present, the client may at some point mention to the partner that he thought the meeting lasted 1½ hours. In either case, the discrepancy could be disastrous. You'll never have an opportunity to prove that you were the only one there sober enough to read a clock.

Always say *"Prepared for and* attended meeting with general counsel of client —2 hours." Those three extra words, which don't cost you anything, could make all the difference.

The same principle applies when you've spent all day proofreading hundreds of pages of industrial bond documents. It's not that you did anything wrong; you were *supposed* to spend all day proofreading those things. But dress it up a little. Instead of saying "Proofreading—9 hours," say *"Reviewing, editing, and* proofreading—9 hours." Again, three little words could make a world of difference.

• Before beginning work on any assignment, make sure you understand exactly what the partner wants. This is not as easy as it may sound.

The partner might want an argumentative piece that contains no reference to authority running against the client's position. He might want a general survey of the law, including all authority pro and con. He might initially want the latter, but having read your memo, decide he wants the former, and wonder why you didn't give him something he could use.

Rarely will he *tell* you what he wants. You have to figure it out.

This raises the question of what your immediate response should be with respect to a partner who has not made clear what he wants. Sometimes a partner will present you with an assignment so garbled you will suspect his sobriety.

As a rational person, you will be tempted to ask questions. You will feel an impulse to attempt to clarify the problem and make sure you understand what it is that is desired.

Resist this impulse! One or two questions are okay, three at most, just to let the partner know you're awake and paying attention as he drones on (stifle yawns at all costs).

But no more! Further inquiry, however reasonable, will only make him nervous regarding your intelligence and legal acumen. If he hasn't made the problem clear the first time around, it's probably because he doesn't understand it himself.

Your best approach, even in the face of the most wildly confused assignment, is to smile, nod your head, and murmur "Yes," "I see," and "I understand." When he has finished (as far as you can tell), you should leave the office, find a quiet place to vomit, and then track down a senior associate to find out what the hell is going on.

• Save all your drafts. It doesn't matter whether you're writing a $10 million oil lease, a $500 opinion letter, or a crummy memo to file. If you run it past a partner (and you should), and he makes you do it over ten or twelve times (and he will), save every version. There's at least a 50–50 chance the partner will call you three days later, and say, "By the way, Kyle, you did save those early drafts, didn't you?"

This makes no sense. If you asked the partner why he wanted them, he would say you never know when some of the material from those early drafts might prove useful. But the real reason is that he's scared—not of anything in particular; just scared, like a kid at night who calls his father to shine the flashlight under the bed.

By all means resist pointing out to the partner the absurdity of his request. Humor him. Tell him you've saved every scrap, and they're all just waiting for the time when they might be needed. And make sure they are: you never know when he'll show up with a flashlight to check under the bed.

• Make four times as many copies of every document as you can possibly use. This is particularly true with respect to litigation briefs, for which you will need:

• an original and three copies (for actual filing);

• another copy that the court clerk will "file stamp" and return to you so you can prove to the partners that you actually filed it;

• "service copies," *i.e.,* copies for you to serve upon (or deliver to) all opposing lawyers;

• intra-office copies (send one to *every* lawyer who had anything at all to do with producing the brief, and one to the partner who brought in the client);

• client copies (send copies to *everyone* at the client's offices who you ever talked to or heard might have an interest in the case);

• your own copy;

• fifteen copies for people you have never heard of, but who will materialize out of the woodwork as soon as you have filed the documents, asking for copies which they will never read;

• ten copies to replace the other copies that will turn out to have missing pages or that your secretary will have used to clean gum off the bottom of her shoe;

• ten copies just to have around, so you can truthfully answer in the affirmative when a partner asks if you made some extra copies in case of an emergency.

This last point is particularly true. If you do not make a ridiculous number of extra copies, the partner in charge will find out and be irritated that you did not make a ridiculous number of extra copies.

Also, and most often overlooked, you should get the client to sign *several* copies of everything you may need to file that requires the client's signature. The concern is that if the original is lost, someone will have to crawl to the client for a second signing. This is crazy, of course, and savvy clients who recognize ass covering for what it is will be irritated. There is a better than even

Make extra copies of everything! It could save your legal career.

chance, however, that some partner will ask if you had the good sense to take this precaution, and you will need the tangible proof at hand.

RULE NO. 2. TAKE ON AS FEW WORK ASSIGNMENTS AS POSSIBLE

This rule may seem inconsistent with what you've heard about the brutal hours associates are required to work, but it isn't. We aren't saying you shouldn't generate some impressive hours, and we *definitely* aren't saying you shouldn't *appear* to be working extremely hard. (*See* Rule No. 4.)

We *are* saying that your goal should be to do a *great* job on a *few* projects, rather than a so-so job on a *great number* of projects. Mediocre reviews can be fatal in this highly competitive field, no matter how early in your career they slip into your file.*

---

* Don't worry about having a small number of reviews, if they're good. Leonardo da Vinci completed only seven paintings; Snickenberger did hundreds.

REINING IN THE
PARTNER

A critical skill every associate needs to develop is that of preventing the partner with whom you're working from saying something foolish or just plain wrong in front of a client.

Partners tend to bluff a lot in client meetings, and sometimes a partner goes too far. Maybe he doesn't know the terrain, or maybe he's just feeling good and gets carried away. Whatever, he starts giving advice that you know could send the client into bankruptcy or prison.

Your job in this situation is to stop him.

Doing so requires alertness, because you have to see quickly where the partner is going and cut him off before he reaches the point of no return.

It also requires diplomacy, because you have to intervene without exceeding too far the limits of your humble station. (You're there only because the partner likes an audience or might want coffee.)

One approach is to interrupt him in mid-sentence:

Mr. Petersmeyer, I can see you're about to present another of your typically brilliant ideas, but

Why would anyone give you a mediocre review, you may justly wonder, if you're doing decent work while carrying a heroic workload? Why wouldn't the partners take the sheer volume of your work into account, and how could they expect the usual level of perfection from an associate who is doing the work of four?

In this regard, it is critical to note three points about how law firms work. First, partners are no less selfish perhaps we should first explain to Ms. Quale the more conventional approach, so she'll know what her competitors are doing.

If the outrageous proposal is already on the table, you could say,

Another way to achieve the same objective—you explained this to me just yesterday, Mr. Petersmeyer—would be to . . .

Either of these displays of uncommon boldness on your part will probably startle the partner, like a bucket of cold water, into recognizing what he was about to do. At that point he will follow up with,

Huh? . . . Oh . . . Yes . . . Yes, absolutely. We could do that, too. Options, Ms. Quale. We want you to know all the options.

The partner won't love you for this, because he'll feel foolish about it. He definitely won't thank you for covering his ass.

But don't let the certainty of his ingratitude prevent you from helping him out.

Remember: whenever a partner looks foolish, an associate's head rolls.

than anyone else on the street, and they are extremely attuned to covering their individual asses. (*See* Rule No. 1.) They don't care about your work for anyone *else*. Each one will expect perfection from you on *his* assignment, and if he doesn't get perfection, he will (a) resent it, and (b) remember it.

Second, almost never does one partner in a law firm have any idea as to what demands another partner may be making on you. They operate in black boxes, isolated from each other (and often the world). It is fatal to assume that partners communicate with each other, and that they will not make conflicting demands on your time: they don't, and they will.

Third, it is a verity that partners have short memories with respect to associates' contributions to the firm as a whole. Your overall performance may have been superlative in view of the number of balls you were juggling at one time, but you can be certain that a few years and even a few months down the road, anyone who may once have known the full story will have long since forgotten it.

Undoubtedly your spartan sacrifices will win you points in the eyes of the Deity. But when partnership evaluation time rolls around, those baggy-eyed months when you foreswore sex and averaged three hours of sleep per night will mysteriously disappear from the collective partnership memory.

This problem of conflicting demands made on associates is hardly of recent vintage. Indeed, having heard of it repeatedly over the years

from involuntarily departing associates, partners at most firms are prepared with two facile responses of which you should be aware.

First, they say, associates are expected to act as "professionals," *i.e.,* to do top quality work on *everything* they undertake. As a practical matter, this is utterly unresponsive to the problem of conflicting demands on associates' time. Nevertheless, partners continue to hoist the ill defined, self-promoting, semi-macho banner of "professionalism" with respect to a number of irrational expectations.

The second reply partners make with respect to the problem of conflicting demands is that associates should be mature enough to protect themselves. In this regard, take them at their word: C.Y.A. Make sure your butt is covered but good.

This is easier said than done. The safest and most frequently available approach is to pit the partners against each other, relying on their varying levels of seniority to resolve the problem. Thus, when all your available time

"Let's not concern yourself with partnership, son . . . 'A man's reach should exceed his grasp or what's a heaven for?'"

is being used on a project for Senior Partner Wescoe, and Middle Level Partner Goetz approaches you for help, your response should be no less obsequious and yet self-protecting than the following:

Goetz: "Son, I'd like you to help me draft a prospectus for an offering of convertible debentures that the local power authority plans to offer next week."

You: "That certainly sounds interesting. I enjoy drafting prospectuses and have long been fascinated by the special challenges presented by the interface of federal securities laws and local power regulation. May I assume you have already spoken with Mr. Wescoe, who said he wanted my full attention devoted to his wife's will for the next two months?"

DO YOU HAVE TO
TAKE THE ASSIGNMENT?

Occasionally an associate is asked to work on a project he finds particularly odious—not just tedious or boring (that's to be expected), but repugnant for ideological or other personal reasons. Maybe it involves representing the Ayatollah Khomeini. Or James Watt. Whatever, you couldn't stomach it.

Do you have to do it?

No. But you don't have to remain employed at your firm, either. Turning down a project is risky business.

Actually, you *can* get out of bad projects. But moral reasons don't count. Tell the partner you're doing a number on some *other* segment of the proletariat. Say, "I'd love to help you turn that family out on the street, but I'm already busy breaking this labor union."

Whatever you do, don't attempt to explain your true views to the partner who does the gruesome work. He knows people hate him for what he does, and he's hypersensitive to criticism. This is simply no place for candor.

There's a lot of ugly work floating around at the top firms, because the clients who can afford to pay them didn't

Goetz: "Wescoe, eh? Let me get back in touch with you. I think maybe I can find someone else."

You: "Let me know if there is any way I can help. I had no plans for this Saturday evening that couldn't be rescheduled for next month."

Note that the only people you can interplead in this manner are partners. Law firms aren't like poker, in which two deuces are better than one ace. In law, one partner tops four associates.

RULE NO. 3.
THERE IS NO SUCH
THING AS A "DRAFT"

In legal circles, some words and expressions beget rich by being nice guys. If you don't like wearing a black hat, you should consider a different job.

"A little advice, son. Practice the courage of your convictions outside the office."

come altered through usage. They take on peculiar meanings, remote from popular understanding. They become what are known in the law as "terms of art."

One important term of art is the word "draft." Failure to understand its specialized meaning has left many an eager and capable associate consigned to proofreading loan agreements for the duration (short) of his stay with his firm.

The potential disaster of misunderstanding the term "draft" will confront you early in your career: a partner for whom you've been researching an issue asks you to provide him with a "draft" of a memorandum or brief on that point. More often than not he'll camouflage the trap by saying something like "Just get me a *quick* draft," or "Just *whip off* a draft," or even "Just *dictate* a *rough* draft." The emphasized words should trigger flashing red lights in your mind.

The partner who utters these words does not mean them. When he speaks them, he should be disbelieved. There is no correlation between his expression and his intent.

Notwithstanding how your dictionary might define "draft" ("a first or preliminary writing, subject to revision"), and regardless of all your understanding of words acquired through a major in English, a minor in Linguistics, and seven years of Latin, *this partner wants a polished, final product!*

That he asked for a "draft" does not mean he will tolerate typos. That he directed you to produce a "rough" working document does not mean you should not have checked all your citations in advance. That he said "dictate" this piece does not mean he will excuse the absence of captions, headings and subheadings.

Everything you submit to a partner should be suitable for framing. No matter how casual the request, how insignificant the task, or how few the dollars at issue, the test you should apply to everything bearing your name is its suitability for hanging in the Sistine Chapel of legal documents.

You should note that the communication problem exemplified by partners' consistent misuse of the word draft occurs in a variety of contexts. Two other notable examples are: "Just skim the cases," and "Take a quick look at the law in this area."

Never should an associate "skim" anything, and *never* should an associate take a "quick look" at anything. If you miss one case that is even colorably relevant, or one statute just arguably germane, it will haunt you five years down the road.

A last word regarding "drafts" and other preliminary undertakings: if, in the direst of circumstances, you find yourself unable to complete the exhaustive, perfect work you now know is expected, do not forget Rule No. 1: C. Y. A.

The best way to do this is to state the limits of your work in a memorandum accompanying your product. In such a cover memo, do not hesitate to say,

"In the following discussion, I have, as requested, addressed liability under Securities and Exchange Commission Rule 10b-5. *I have not addressed the question of damages in connection with such liability.*"

Note the emphasized second sentence. Although spineless, it serves to shift the burden higher up for any catastrophic problems that occur. It suggests, without actually saying so, that there was an *understanding* that you would limit your research as stated.

"This will require some creative thinking . . ."

When a partner misuses the word draft, you can protect yourself—*if* you've read this book and know what he really means. Lots of times, however, a partner will say something that signals danger but there's nothing you can do about it—nothing, that is, short of throwing up on his desk to cut him off before the axe falls.

In some instances this will prove to have been a moderate response.

Set forth below are several serious danger signals that associates should recognize for what they are.

1. "This project will require some creative thinking . . ."

The partner who approaches you with these words is cunning. He is about to present you with a problem that he knows has no solution.

Sometimes a client wants to do something he just can't do. Like pave over Lake Tahoe to build a condo complex. Sometimes a client *doesn't* want to do something that the law says he *has* to do. Like pay taxes. Or alimony.

Whatever the problem, the partner will come to you for a solution.

This is one of the more craven things a partner will do. He *knows* there's no solution because he's thought about it and couldn't come up with one—which is what led him to the remark about creative thinking.

Even if you *could* come up with a solution, he

wouldn't use it, because there's no authority for it. If there were any authority, he'd know.

This partner is covering his ass. He'd rather you be the one who failed to come up with a solution, in case he has to explain it to an even more senior partner or to the partner who brought in the client.

If he *is* the partner who brought in the client, or the senior-most partner of the firm, he's covering his ass anyway, out of sheer instinct. After all, that's what got him where he is.

2. "Have you ever done any work on _____?" [Insert "Arkansas contract law," "condo conversion restrictions," "FCC cellular communications regulations."]

The partner who asks this question does not care about the answer. If your answer is no, he will say, "Fine, you're about to get into the area." If your answer is yes, he will say "Fine, we're going to take advantage of your expertise."

His question is rhetorical. It is an indirect way of saying you're about to tackle the most God-awful area of law known to man. He is jus-

tifiably squeamish about presenting the assignment head-on.

3. "Are you busy?"

Your answer to this question should always be "Very busy."

Whoever asks this question is planning to give you an assignment, probably a bad one or he wouldn't have approached you obliquely with the question. (If he approaches you with the even more oblique query, "How are you fixed for time?" you can be sure the assignment has four legs and barks.)

If your answer is merely "Busy," you will get the assignment. You may get it even with "Very busy," but that way you'll at least gain points for carrying a heavy load.

If in fact you're not busy and you think you need the hours, your answer should be the same, but with a qualifier (preferably couched in language suggestive of your heroic capacity for toil): "Very busy, but perhaps I could *shoulder* some more."

4. "This is just a one-day project."

This lie ranks up there with "The check is in the mail," "I'll respect you in the morning," and "It's only a cold sore."

There is no such thing as a one-day project, at least not one they'd bother calling in a new person to work on. If it were really a one-day project, they'd do it themselves.

"One-day" projects usually involve searches for a case or rule that does not exist. Most likely the people in charge have already checked the obvious sources and found nothing. Because your search will turn up nothing, too, you will be required to continue it for days on end, wasting incredible amounts of time as you descend the ladder of obscure sources.

5. "Familiarize yourself with the law in this area."

The partner who says this is setting you up for a fall. He doesn't mean you should merely find out what U.S. Code volume contains the statute he's referring to. He doesn't mean you should become just roughly conversant with the concepts and structure of the law. He's using "familiarize" in the way only partners use it: to *master* an area; to commit to memory every case and every clause in every statute.

It may be that he's got wind of a fast-breaking deal, or he anticipates a dramatic turn of events in a big case. Whatever, he thinks it'll happen fast, or he wouldn't have given you even the little warning that he did. Moreover, he thinks the area is too complicated to be responsible for it himself. He wants someone else's neck on the line: yours.

RULE NO. 4. CULTIVATE THE IMAGE OF A WORKHORSE

In law, appearance is reality.

This rule mandates affirmative craftiness and calculation. It exhorts you to be resourceful and creative in your quest for the proper image.

To assist you in this quest, set forth below are some lifesaving (and marriage-saving) tips on how to maintain the preferred image while keeping your work load under control. These tips fall into five categories:

(a) Setting Your Workload: The Proper Measure

Let's start with a fundamental fact: *billings are important for your career*. Even at the firms that advertise themselves as "laid back" and "full of individuals who value their lives outside the law,"* the partners' greatest lament is that there are only 24 hours in an associate's day. The fact is that in a law firm, some level of work is unavoidable.

But *what* level? The answer to this question depends on your peers at the firm: for appearance's sake, you're going to have to spend roughly as much time working as they do.

But only *roughly* as much! This brings us to one of the major things we can say to ease your burden: do not so much as consider trying to lead your class in billable hours. Not even if it's a small class.

For one thing, you won't be able to do it. There are always a few superhuman grinds around.

In any event, that's not

how *you* want to spend your life. You want more on your tombstone than "G. Mackay Smith, Partner." You'd like at least enough spare time to be able to show up for your own divorce.

The only goal you should set for yourself in this area is to avoid the anchor position in your class. That's good enough. For once in your life, as contrary as it is to your nature, be average.

(b) Easy Hours: How To Beef Up Your Billings Legitimately

Given that you're going to have to chalk up some hours, you should take every possible advantage of the few easy but legitimate ways of beefing up your billings.

Most of your work will not be easy. It will consist of something like researching U.S. Postal regulations, drafting motions for enlargement of time (only a lawyer would attempt to "enlarge" time), or comparing the Delaware nonprofit corporation law to that of the other states, Puerto Rico, Guam, and Louisiana.

Such work is boring (you will find yourself filling out time sheets for fun) and tedi-

---

* What these firms are "full of" is something quite different—and much better for plant growth.

ous (the mental equivalent of needlepoint). It has been compared to digging ditches through a minefield, which doesn't take much intelligence and isn't glamorous or enjoyable, but you have to pay close attention to what you're doing.

When something easy comes your way, pounce on it. Of the various easy but legitimate ways of beefing up your billings, at least three will be available no matter where you work.

Travel

The first, and best, of these is travel. A shrewd associate will involve himself in work for Sri Lankan or New Caledonian clients, preferably corporate work that could entail trips to the company headquarters. The time spent en route to these places is billable, and it is a piece of cake from your point of view. Sure, you *might* have to spend the travel time reviewing client papers—or you *might* have to order a double Jack Daniels and watch *Rocky III* on the airplane movie.

GETTING AWAY FROM IT ALL

Projects that get you out of the office are not to be taken for granted. Better yet are projects that not only get you out of the office but get you someplace where it doesn't matter how you're dressed.

Even if this means going to a law school library to perform a 50-state survey of local franchise laws, or to a client's warehouse to rummage through boxes of ancient records, you will come to relish any opportunity to shed those suit pants (which never fit quite right anyway), that absurd tie (whose only function is to collect tangible evidence of your meals), or those accursed pantyhose (which only make it hard to go to the bathroom).

NOTE: if you're wearing the absurd tie *and* the accursed pantyhose, being stuck in the office isn't your primary problem.

NON-BILLABLE TIME

Non-billable time (also known as "administrative" time) includes such activities as recruiting, running the summer clerk program, doing *pro bono* work, and writing articles and speeches that partners will take credit for. Such time raises a number of questions: Do partners look favorably on *pro bono* work? Do they appreciate all the time you spend writing those speeches for Partner Knopman? Is being put in charge of the summer program a big honor?

The bottom line is: no. At best, these things won't significantly *harm* your chances of partnership.

This is particularly true with respect to *pro bono* work. Regardless of what they may tell you when you're interviewing, partners view *pro bono* work as a form of private charity. Their attitude is: "We don't care if you want to do it, but do it on your own time."

"We practice law to make money, Hawkins . . . if you have a more compelling reason to practice law, let's hear it."

The same is true for speeches and articles Most of these won't even bear your name, and the few partners who once knew you were the author won't remember it three months later.

As for being appointed to run the summer program, most associates view this not only as an honor heralding a glorious future with the firm but also as a daily opportunity for a free lunch.

There is no such thing as a free lunch. While you're playing camp counsellor, your peers are meeting clients and developing expertise. *They're* becoming lawyers.

What about the honor of being appointed to such a high profile position? Don't be naïve. Either your substantive work is more dispensable than anyone else's, or you're such a grind that the partners know you'll eat the time—you'll run the program during the day and keep your billables up in the evenings and on Sundays. (On Saturdays you'd be working anyway.)

Don't let anyone give you the runaround about how such work builds "goodwill" and "appreciation" around the firm. Half the partners think summer clerks should be treated with kid gloves, and half think they should be made to earn their keep; no matter how you run the program, at least half will think you screwed up.

Besides, if they really appreciate it, they'll reward it with cash. In this regard your motto should be: "Let others have the 'goodwill.' Give me the dough."

Defending Depositions

The second source of easy hours involves defending depositions. This means accompanying your client to respond to some other lawyer's demand that your client answer questions about a lawsuit. All *you* have to do is sit still and listen.

To make your client feel secure (you're there in a sort of hand-holding capacity) and to prevent yourself from falling asleep, you should object periodically to the line of questioning, whatever it is. This means challenging it on grounds of "form" (how it's worded) or "relevance" (what it has to do with any-thing).

If the client is a key wit-ness in a big-money case, it's a good idea to pay attention. You'll never encounter that situation as an associate, however, so don't worry about it now.

Proofreading

Finally, there are easy hours to be had in proofread-ing. Every writing that leaves the firm has to be proofread. The partners expect it to be done, and the clients expect, however grudgingly, to pay for it.

You don't want to find yourself proofreading too often: it's boring, and it looks silly on your resumé as your primary field of expertise. Still, proofreading has the prime virtue that frequently you can arrange to do it *at home,* stretched out on your sofa in your underwear eating Doritos and listening to Vi-valdi or Willie Nelson. Also, catching a few typos that everyone else has missed (a "catch," in legal parlance— for example, "Nice catch, Otis. I didn't see that.") can earn big points in the eyes of the partner overseeing the project.

(c) Weekend Work: Avoiding It, Simulating It

A legal career inevitably involves weekend work. It was a lawyer who said, "Thank God it's Friday— only two more work days until Monday."

A question confronting all associates is how to know when weekend work is really necessary. Legal work is like school work, in that you could always do more in a given area. (Or like psycho-analysis, in that the more you get into it, the uglier things look.)

Your goal, of course, is to minimize weekend work. Free weekends are what it's all about.

To keep your Saturdays and Sundays as carefree as possible, keep in mind that weekend work is of two types. First, there is serious, big-time work that has been brewing for a long time. It could be a major antitrust suit that you've been involved in, the papers are due on Mon-day, and you are, by any test, the logical person to spend the necessary weekend time buffing up the brief.

There is no escape from such work. You should resign yourself to it, exploiting the opportunities it will afford to enhance your image as a hard worker. If the partner in charge takes the extraordinary step of *asking* whether you will be able to help out over the weekend, and you have sized up the situation and see that you are clearly the logical choice for the job, *do it!*

Pretend you are *glad* about it. Tell him you were already *planning* to be there.

Tell him you *like* weekends because they give you a chance to hunker down without a lot of interruptions from the secretaries. (Do not worry about your credibility in this regard: lots of partners really *do* like weekends for that very reason.)

Above all, do not make him order you to be there. He will do it, so you won't have gained anything. But he will not like doing it. Once you've started rubbing his conscience the wrong way or convinced him that you're

"Too busy? Oh, no sir, I'm not too busy . . . my desire to Shepardize knows no bounds."

not a team player, you might as well ease on down the road.

The second type of weekend work is emergency work: short-term, last-minute, run-of-the-mill work that any associate could do. *This* type of work you can avoid.

This isn't *your* emergency; it isn't something they need *you* to handle. It might be that a judge has just asked some partner to brief an issue by Monday, or the local prosecutor has just summoned a client of the firm to appear before a grand jury.

More likely, some partner hasn't bothered taking care of a matter that has been around for a long time, because he knew there was a full stable of associates he could get to handle it at the last minute.

Any associate can handle these types of emergencies, and you shouldn't be concerned about the propriety of

FRIDAY AFTERNOONS
(The art of laying low)

Friday afternoon is a critical time. That's when partners start checking their calendars to see what's on tap for Monday; that's when your weekend stands its greatest chance of being destroyed.

Try to avoid answering your phone over these hours. Definitely do not check with your secretary or receptionist for messages. (Once either of these has told you some partner is looking for you, you're caught. No support staffer can be trusted to hide the fact that you don't return calls on Friday afternoons.)

Avoid walking past any partners' offices on the way to the restroom. If possible, don't even *go* to the restroom over these hours. If you absolutely have to, consider finding a nice stall and staying there the entire afternoon.

Ideally you should arrange to be out of the building altogether; an appointment with your chiropractor will do. If that isn't possible, the next best strategy is to set up camp in an obscure corner of the library. Just take your books and papers and whatever you're working trying to avoid them. What you should be concerned about is *how* to avoid them. It can be done. *See* "Friday Afternoons," below.

You might well wonder about the costs of such an approach. Won't people get angry if you consistently manage to avoid weekend work? Most likely, no one will know. No one keeps a list of weekends worked. Still, it's worth covering your ass here, as everywhere.

There are three especially handy devices for doing this.

First, many firms have a receptionist come in for all or part of each Saturday. This affords you a great opportunity. Whether you are at home, at the beach, or at a friend's place on Saturday morning engaged in some horizontal recreation, set the alarm for about 11:00 A.M., sit up, call the office and, using a false voice, have yourself paged.

on with you. Don't worry about how it looks; lots of people keep mountains of garbage there.

Be sure it's an *obscure* corner of the library. Not infrequently, a partner needing bodies will actually prowl through the library in search of hapless associates for weekend duty. Also, you want to be able to ignore your name when it goes out over the paging system; if you're in a crowded area some jerk will tap you on the shoulder to say he thinks he just heard your name.

What about matters you actually need to handle over these hours? Use the library phone to call your date regarding weekend plans. Everything else can wait until Monday.

Everyone who is really at the office will assume you are there, too, somewhere. That they haven't seen you won't matter; law firms are big places. And don't worry that the receptionist will know you haven't answered your page; she doesn't care.

Why 11:00 A.M.? Most people who work on Saturday do so in the morning, so if you call later you might miss them, as well as the receptionist.

On the other hand, the really senior people who come in surely won't do so *before* 11:00 A.M., so you don't want to call too early.

Besides, it *is* the weekend.

Another handy device for simulating weekend work is more effective but also more demanding. It involves actually going in.

This doesn't have to ruin your picnic plans. You don't have to *stay* there. Just go in, look a bit fatigued (not *too* fatigued; you're supposed to be able to take the pressure), walk briskly through the library, grab two or three reference volumes, return to your office, turn on the light, and then head for the links.

Turning on your light is important. The cleaning personnel will have turned off all office lights on Friday evening, so anyone who sees your light burning on Saturday thinks you've been in.

The joy of this trick is that it keeps working all weekend. In most office buildings the cleaning personnel won't be around again until Monday night, so you get the benefit through Saturday evening, all Sunday, and even Monday at dawn.

Turning your light on after the cleaning personnel have passed is a trick capable of application during the week in many firms. If the cleaners make their rounds past your office around 7:00 P.M. most evenings, and you happen to finish your squash game at the gym next door at 7:30 P.M., stop by and turn on your light. It can't hurt your image for those who pass by later that night or the few who come in early the next day.

As long as you're in on any weekend, consider leaving some kind of note on the desk of a partner, just to let him know you were in. You have to be careful with this device, because it can be a bit transparent. Don't do it *every* weekend, and don't write in red ink at the top of the note "SATURDAY, 7:00 P.M." Let the partner figure out when the note must have been written, as by observing that it was written on the back of that weekend's church bulletin.

The third method of simulating weekend work requires you to ingratiate yourself with the guard stationed at your office building on weekends. With flattery and a bottle of scotch, you may be able to persuade him to sign your name on the check-in list that office buildings maintain on Saturdays and Sundays.

All those who actually come by will see your name as they sign their own names. Better yet, they *won't* see a mark beside your name in the check-*out* column—clear evidence that you've outlasted them all.

The only danger with this trick is that others may be doing the same thing. If fifteen associates' names appear in alphabetical order in identical script, someone may sense a sham.

(d) All-Nighters

All-night work has much in common with weekend work: it's unpleasant and should be minimized, but it gives you an excellent opportunity to enhance your image as a hard worker.

Like death, all-nighters cannot be avoided indefinitely. When your number comes up, remember two points: (a) do it gracefully, and (b) don't keep it a secret.

The first point is of primary importance. Because everyone has to pull an all-nighter at some time, no one is going to feel sorry for you. If you bitch about it, you won't even get credit for your dedication, because everyone will know you did it involuntarily.

The preferred posture is one of ease and nonchalance. This suggests that you are possessed of unusual stamina. (Let your colleagues think you wouldn't even go to bed but for social reasons.)

It also suggests that you do this sort of thing *all the time,* which carries the further implication that other, more senior persons view you as the person to call upon in a crunch, the "can do" guy. Over time, it will have partners and associates alike believing that you get called in for the *hard* cases.

The only problem is that your Hemingwayesque grace under pressure will be wasted if no one knows about it. Hence, the second point: don't keep your all-nighter a secret.

In practice, this point can conflict with the goal of handling the all-nighter gracefully. Talking about it is inconsistent with shrugging it off as commonplace. Thus you should make considerable efforts not to pull your all-nighters alone. With someone else present, the word of your energy and stamina will spread.

"Dudley here just pulled his first all-nighter . . . brings back some great memories, doesn't it?"

The All-Nighter. Prolonged sleep deprivation can produce anxiety and insecurity in even the sturdiest associate.

If you cannot finagle company for the duration, do not despair. You can make your exertions known to the partner in charge of the project by showing up in his office the next day wearing the same clothes you were wearing the day before.

When doing this, you should make sure that your clothes are orderly (shirt tucked in, belt buckled, brassiere facing forward), because you don't want to look out of control. However, your shirt should be suitably wrinkled, and your beard shadow suitably dark (particularly impressive on women) —these things you can't be expected to do anything about.

Another reason you should not be too distressed by the absence of company for your all-nighter is that when you're alone you can take naps on conference room sofas. Before lying down on that sofa, however, take the precaution of arranging for a trusted friend (preferably someone outside the firm) to ring the conference room telephone early the next morning. It's professionally embarrassing to be caught blowing big league Z's when you're supposed to be polishing up a brief.

(e) General Image Tips

Keep your secretary busy.

This is especially important if you share a secretary with a partner. The partner will gauge your productivity from your secretary's pace.

If you are sharing a secretary with a partner, none of your work will get done. The secretary will use the partner's work as a pretext to avoid yours so she can finish the latest issue of *Cosmopolitan*. She isn't there to *work* eight hours a day—at least not for some lowlife associate.

Nevertheless you must make the effort.

One way to give the impression of keeping your secretary busy is to keep her "In" box loaded with papers. What kind of papers doesn't matter. If you need one letter copied, attach that letter to two or three large files and leave the whole stack in her box. The partner will see the stack and be impressed.

Another way to generate a large volume of material for your secretary's "In" box is to use a separate cassette for each letter or memo you dictate. With one hour's labor on Monday morning, you can produce enough tapes to suggest a whole weekend of work.

Some particularly impor-

tant image tips relate to those occasions when you need to go home a little early—say, around lunchtime.

This will occur once in a while. You have a lot going on in your life. You need the time to keep your affairs in order.

That's cool. But C.Y.A.

You can do this in several ways. First, always leave by the stairwell rather than the elevator. Even if you're on the 40th floor. A partner who sees you boarding the "down" elevator will be suspicious, no matter how full your briefcase or purposeful your stride. (By all means carry a briefcase, not your squash racquet.)

Next, prepare for the calls that might come in after you've gone. You don't want partners being told you went home after a half day.

Tell your secretary or receptionist, whoever will get the calls in your absence, that you're off to a meeting (you don't need to say *which* meeting). Say you'll be back when it's over, but it might not end until after the office closes. The point you want to convey is that although she might not see you again until tomorrow, she should tell

Signs of Life

1. *Light burning brightly. (Tape the light switch in the "on" position, so the clean-up crew won't flip it off in your absence.)*
2. *Coat on back of chair.*
3. *Uncapped pen.*
4. *Full cup of coffee. (Make sure it's full. Half-cups are common.)*
5. *Smoking cigarette. (Check your local novelty store for those Permalite cigarettes that give off smoke for hours.)*
6. *Half-eaten sandwich. (How long could you last on a half-empty stomach?)*
7. *Phone with blinking "Hold" button. (Dial your home phone, which will ring until you get in from your night on the town, and punch the "Hold" button and leave.)*
8. *Open Federal Reporter.*
9. *Shoes. (How far could you get without your shoes?)*
10. *Open briefcase. (Keep a second one around for this purpose. You should be carrying your first one with you when you leave.)*
11. *Open drawer. (Partners are too fastidious to believe you'd leave it that way all night.)*
12. *Legal pad with writing cut off in mid-sentence . . . even mid-word.*

callers that you've gone "out," not that you've gone "home."

(If you're worried that a partner who gets this message might work late that night and wonder why he didn't see you around, call in for messages after nine holes. Otherwise, just be prepared the next day to say that because of where the meeting was held, it was more efficient to stay there to finish reviewing "the papers" (there are always papers) than to return to the office.

What about partners who stop by your office and see no signs of life? Make sure there *are* signs of life.

Your light should be on, of course.

But go the extra mile. Leave a suit coat in plain view, on the back of your chair or the arm of your sofa. Shrewd associates keep an extra coat constantly on hand for this purpose.*

Also, leave a full cup of coffee on your desk. Lawyers make a lot of money, but they just can't believe someone would waste a full cup of coffee.

* Be sure you leave a suit *coat*, not suit *pants*. The implications are entirely different.

In your quest for the image of a workhorse, keep in mind that you can score big points by being in the right place at the right time. If your firm's Administrative Committee meets over coffee and doughnuts every Thursday at 7:30 A.M., find some excuse for strolling by their conference room every Thursday at 7:30 A.M.—with your sleeves already rolled up and your hair *not* still wet from your morning shower.

The same principle applies on days when the weather is so bad that public transportation ceases to operate, and three-fourths of the secretaries call in swearing their cars won't start. Sometimes you can predict these disasters in advance (as when you're in Atlanta and the evening news predicts heavy dew).

In such situations, set your alarm for what will seem like the middle of the night, and make an all-out effort to get to the office by 7:00 A.M. Invariably, one or two supremely hard-boiled partners will have done the same thing, motivated by white collar machismo to be able to tell their friends the storm

didn't keep them from the office.

When they see you there early, they will recognize you as one of "their kind of guy." They won't commend you—you're only doing what you're expected to do. But they'll remember it and always think better of you than of your lightweight candy-assed colleagues who weakened when the going got tough.

A final tip on cultivating the proper image: never leave your office without a book or yellow pad in hand. It doesn't matter that you're just going to the bathroom. It doesn't matter that no one can see what you're carrying (it might as well be *Our Bodies, Ourselves*). You're after the proper *image*. Over the years, subsconsciously, partners will come to associate you with the implements of labor. That association will help carry you where you want to go.

RULE NO. 5. AVOID PERIPHERAL INVOLVEMENT IN ANYTHING

Every now and then you will be called upon to perform a small task in connection with a large project. The partner in charge will assure you that your time commitment will be minimal and that your end of the work will be both interesting and educationally valuable.

Use any excuse to avoid this task. It can only bring you misery.

Your work will not be interesting. No case is so interesting that it cannot be broken down into boring pieces, and the premise of your involvement is that you will be working on one of the most subordinate pieces.

Neither will your work be educationally valuable. No one will explain to you the background of the case, or bother to keep you informed as to its progress. You will work in an absolute void—not dissimilar from what your social life has become since you joined the firm.

That the work will be boring and educationally worthless is the least of your problems. *Lots* of your work will be boring and educationally worthless.

The main problem is the enormous potential for damage to your reputation. Once

"He read my memo. Then he told me ignorance of the law was no excuse."

you have done anything on a case, people assume you know everything there is to know about it, and they think you an imbecile for not having every one of its details at your fingertips.

They forget the limited nature of your original exposure and are irritated by your lack of comprehension. The fact that you don't know what is going on is not rendered forgivable in their eyes by the fact that no one has *told* you what is going on.

To add insult to injury, you are forever after "on call" for emergencies requiring weekend work and all-nighters in connection with the case. In big cases, emergencies occur all the time, and an associate who has done as little as fifteen minutes of work on such a case is considered to have special responsibilities with respect to its most onerous tasks.

This problem of peripheral involvement in a large case is not unlike that of becoming marginally familiar with an objectionable area of the law. Once you have so much as glimpsed the Federal Submerged Lands Act, or even stubbed your toe on the U.S. Code volume containing it, you are forever after deemed the firm's expert on that subject. Buying a stamp at the post office qualifies you as your firm's expert on U.S. Postal Regulations.

The lesson? Scope out all projects in advance. Where possible, avoid those that strike you as odious, regardless of how minor your involvement is promised to be. Your willingness to play the role of the courteous dinner guest, cheerfully consuming whatever slop is put before you, will only bring you second, third and fourth helpings of the same.

RULE NO. 6. GIVE THE PARTNERS SOMETHING PRACTICAL

If you want to succeed as an associate, shed all pretensions of scholarship. Practicing law is a trade. Notwithstanding what you learned in law school, a lawyer is like a garage mechanic, only he charges more because he wears a tie.

Lawyers like to think of themselves as scholars. It's how they explain to themselves why they don't earn as much as businesspeople.

Nevertheless, what partners want out of you when they ask for a memorandum is something they can insert wholesale into a brief or send directly to the client.

This doesn't mean your product should be readable. You *are* a lawyer.

But it should not be a Law Review article. If you produce a think-piece or an academic treatise, they'll make you do it again.

No doubt this will frustrate you. Throughout law school, the professors emphasized the scholarly aspects of law. You learned that writing for your school's Law Review and reaching impossible conclusions was where it's at.

Ignore all that. Satisfying clients is what the partners are trying to do. Satisfying partners is what you're trying to do.

RULE NO. 7. DO NOT DIP YOUR PEN IN THE COMPANY INKWELL

This colloquial rendering of the traditional taboo on intraoffice dating has been expressed in other ways as well. Most notable is the "hamburger rule," which forbids obtaining your meat where you obtain your bread.

Every firm has at least one lecherous senior partner. More often than not, this person is male. Lecherous *female* senior partners are not common features of the legal landscape—the profession is not so advanced.

This lecher may or may not be single. He may or may not be attractive.

He is, invariably, smooth and confident. He will sit down in your office, cross his legs and straighten his tie in a slick way that says here, at last, is a guy who really knows how to sit down, cross his legs and straighten his tie.

What should you realize, if you find yourself attracted by his act, is that you won't be *sharing* it; you'll be *adorning* it. Another notch on his bedpost.

And let there be no question: he has lust on his mind, as well as in his heart.

He may come on subtly: "You know, your eyes are as blue as my Ferrari."

Or he may be more direct: "How about brunch on Sunday? Come by early, say, Saturday night."

However the liaison begins, experience suggests it won't last. Afterwards, you'll be just another source of smirks among the support staff.

It may occur to you that such a liaison will promote your career. Don't be naïve. For each lover/partner who *may* become an ally in your fight for advancement, you'll acquire 40 enemies among your fellow associates, who will have a thousand opportunities to torpedo you along the already perilous passage to partnership.

Even if your ally is a Big Gun in the firm, his clout will not be enough at partnership time to offset the hostility of the other partners. They will scorn you for what they will perceive as an obvious ploy. They will be jealous that one of their colleagues is having more fun than they are.

With respect to "horizontal integration," *i.e.,* associates dating other associates, the dangers are substantially lessened. Your motives are less suspect because the alliance does not enhance your competitve position.

The major problem with dating another associate is what happens after you break up. If you part ways on unfriendly terms, you will still have to see each other every day in the library. You will have to suffer in silence as he or she shows up at the Christmas formal with a new date. (Scratching her eyes out, or kicking him in the groin, is considered unprofessional outside of Texas.)

Perhaps the best policy

with respect to any form of intraoffice dating is, in legal jargon, a "rebuttable presumption against." It is *presumed* that you will not become involved in an intraoffice affair, the costs *usually* being too high, but this presumption can be *rebutted* in certain special cases.

For females, such special cases have been called the "Tom Selleck exception." For males, the "Victoria Principal principle." In these cases, the costs of an affair *can't* outweigh the benefits.

RULE NO. 8. STAY ALERT TO YOUR LONG-TERM PROSPECTS

If you are content at your firm and doing well, there is no reason you should not stick around indefinitely. On the other hand, if you are going to leave your firm (voluntarily or on a rail), you should know that a junior associate enjoys greater mobility with respect to other firms than a senior associate.

This is partly a result of inter-firm competition and pride. The top firms are hy-

"Every firm needs someone like you, Stokes . . . Unfortunately for you, however, our firm already has that someone."

persensitive to the suggestion that they might be willing to take on an associate who didn't "make the grade" elsewhere. (Some of the best credentialed firms are the most insecure in this regard, snubbing "used" associates with a disdain more appropriate for used dental floss.)

Also, firms prefer legal virgins: they feel that a lawyer who has spent time elsewhere has lost something vital.

Finally, a young associ-

THE STAR SYSTEM

Law firms operate on a "star system." Within two or three years after graduation, a few associates are singled out from each class as "stars" of that class. There's no formal awards ceremony, but everyone knows who they are.

Being marked as a star is a self-fulfilling prophecy. Stars receive the best work (such as it is) and the most responsibility—in short, the greatest opportunities to shine.

You don't get to be a star by caring about the outside world. If you've already been designated a star, you probably aren't reading this book.

The big question is: what if you're *not* one of the stars of your class? Do you bail out? Work three times as hard? Sabotage the stars?

If you're sure that being a star is what you want (and to make part-

ner you *have* to be a star), hang in there for a year or two. The fact that you're not a star yet doesn't mean all the slots are permanently filled. Circumstances can cause a star's luster to fade. A star can become a black hole.

Otherwise, resign yourself to second class citizenship and go about your business. Your salary will continue to come in.

More important, you'll acquire a certain peace of mind; once you know you're not going to make partner, you can quit *worrying* about not making partner. You can loosen your collar, take time to read the morning paper, and schedule something for Saturday night. You can treat your work at the firm as a "job" rather than a "career"—the difference is about 30 hours per week.

ate can claim that he was disappointed with his first firm, that it rarely had enough work to keep him going past 8:00 or 9:00 P.M.: "I couldn't stay at a place where they work part-time."

If the problem at a given firm is that *you* don't like *it*, you need be only marginally concerned as to how *it* regards *you*. You don't want to screw up anything so badly that they padlock your office

Mathers there is our rising star . . . billed 2400 hours last year and has set his goals even higher for this year."

tomorrow and give several Doberman pinschers a whiff of your handkerchief, but basically you can walk out whenever you can't take it anymore.

If, on the other hand, you are not unhappy where you are and could imagine yourself still there five or ten years down the road, you need to keep a sharp lookout for indicia of your progress vis-a-vis your peers.

SIGNALS THAT YOU'RE ON YOUR WAY OUT

How can you tell when things aren't going well for you at a firm, that the partners consider you a short-timer, that you're on your way out?

The subtlest of the bad tidings is bad work: your assignments, instead of growing *less* boring and *less* tedious over time, continue to extend the frontiers of "boredom" and "tedium." This is difficult to gauge—normal people find all associate work boring and tedious, and it's tough to know whether yours is more or less so than average.

A somewhat clearer sign is getting The Freezeout: assignments stop coming in at all. At first The Freezeout seems like a blessing—you're thrilled to have your evenings free, and you revel in being able to get together with friends for lunch. Then you realize that your learning curve is plummeting, and you find yourself hating to go into the office because of the whispers you suspect accompany your every step.

Take heart. No longer must you sit in doubt, agonizing over whether the axe is about to fall. Set

There is only one real indicium, although it travels under many names: bread, long green, jack, whipout, scratch, moolah, clams, cabbage, flaps, dough, simoleons —some have been heard to call it money.

You will hear stories of other indicia, such as interesting work, sexy travel, nice office space, or a secretary willing to correct typos. The firms themselves will even tell you to heed your *evaluations,* which most of them provide annually or semiannually and which no associate in his right mind trusts except in negative circumstances (such as when the evaluator demands your office key and asks where you would like them to forward your mail).

But if money isn't everything, it is definitely way ahead of whatever is in second place. If you fall behind the pack in salary (or even fail to stay up with the leaders in a large class), you would forth below are ten clear indicators to watch for, signals that you're on the way out:

1. Your new office has no desk or window, and the chair flushes.

2. The firm librarian requires you to put up collateral each time you take out a book.

3. A partner posts your latest memo on the bulletin board in the secretaries' lounge to give them a laugh.

4. Your annual salary raise is in the four figures, *including* the two after the decimal point.

5. The firm holds its summer outing at the Scarsdale Country Club, but your invitation says "Larry's Mini-Golf and Garage."

6. Your secretary is replaced by a typewriter and a copy of *Porter's Guide to Resumés.*

7. The firm considers you for partnership every three months, just so they can tell you you've been passed over *again.*

8. You find yourself receiving assignments from junior people—including messengers.

9. Instead of a Christmas bonus, you're given a set of luggage.

10. Your client contact is confined to trusts and estates clients whose wills have become effective.

be well advised to start buffing up your resumé.

On Not Making Partner

Even with the aid of this book, there's a chance you won't make partner. Most associates don't.*

* "Figures provided to Columbia [University School of Law] by 10 law firms show that of a total of 246 lawyers from the [law school] class of 1972 who entered these firms, only 33 made partner. Some examples: Cravath, Swaine & Moore, one out of 27; Sullivan & Cromwell, two out of 22; Davis, Polk & Wardwell, two out of 23." *Wall Street Journal,* cover page, January 3, 1983.

Times are hard for law firms these days, and partners are looking for reasons *not* to let you on board, rather than the reverse.

Partnership decisions are said to reflect the Screwee Rule: they'll do it to you if they can. (The only associates they can't afford to screw are those who've either developed their own clients—Young Rainmakers —or shrewdly carved out indispensable areas of expertise.)

"Do you hear me? I was partnership material!"

If you get shot down, ask yourself whether life would have been so great if you'd made it—are those really the people with whom you wanted to spend the rest of your life? Not making partner could be compared to getting bounced from a leper colony: the world outside may be better than what you're leaving.

TEN WAYS TO END A LEGAL CAREER

1. When a partner in your firm announces that his wife is pregnant, distribute a memo denying responsibility.

2. After a brief has been filed, express to the partner in charge your regret that you didn't have time to citecheck the cases.

3. Suggest that conflicts of interest preclude your firm from representing General Motors.

4. Come in to the office at the crack of noon —two days in a row.

5. While defending a client in a deposition, tell him he has to answer the other lawyer's questions truthfully.

6. Explain to a client how the time he's being billed for was really spent.

7. Score with a secretary that a senior partner has been unsuccessfully putting the moves on for months.

8. After jogging to the office one morning, hang your athletic supporter or brassiere on a conference-room doorknob to dry.

9. Fail to read this book.

10. Write this book.

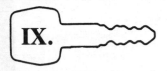

IX

Once You're a Partner
(THE CROCK AT THE END OF THE RAINBOW)

The mere thought of partnership mesmerizes legal associates. They daydream about it, drooling unconsciously like basset hounds remembering old soupbones.

According to associate myth, partnership is a blissful

"Welcome aboard, Hotchkiss. You're one of us now."

143

state, synonymous with Heaven, Paradise, Nirvana, and other realms free of famine, pestilence, war, death, citechecking, and shareholder resolutions. Don't believe it.

Many young lawyers think their lives will change once they become partners. If this is your game plan, ask yourself why partners continue to leave their office lights on when they go home in the middle of the afternoon. Who are they trying to fool?

Ask yourself why part-

"Kelsy, when will you learn that bathroom time, in and of itself, is non-billable?"

ners continue to carry memos and advance sheets into the bathrooms to read at the stand-up urinals.* Who are they trying to impress?

Whether partnership will even approach your fantasies depends on a number of factors, including whether your firm is large or small.

(A) THE SMALL FIRM

The most obvious difference between large firms and small firms is size. Hence the labels "large" and "small." At a small firm, making partner might have only a marginal effect on your life. Consider the following four criteria:

Scut Work

At small firms cases are staffed leanly, usually with just one partner and one associate, so that there are limits on how much of the scut work you can foist onto the associate. Sure, you'll no longer have to do scut work that doesn't need to be done by *anyone,* the tasks that

partners often make associates do because the associates are available and why not. But you'll still have to do *some* scut work—and some is more than you want.

$$

Small firms aren't supported by a proletariat of associates who generate three times as much in client billings as they're paid. Unless you're Clark Clifford, who might make enough from a single well placed phone call to buy an underdeveloped nation, the only yacht you'll be sailing when you make partner at a small firm is the one with the rubber band motor that you still play with in the bathtub.

Job Security

Job security in the law is dependent on clients like I.B.M. and Chase Manhattan Bank that need millions of dollars worth of legal work each year. These clients have mountains of money. They

* Not just the men.

print their own. They're a fantastic gravy train—but only the big firms can climb aboard. Moreover, small firms face the constant and disastrous possibility of a split-off; what do you do if your sole expert on the one-bite rule leaves to set up his own firm specializing in dog law?

Prestige

How great can the prestige be in a small firm? You can't dazzle everyone at cocktail parties, because non-lawyers will never have heard of your firm. Other lawyers will snobbishly assume the competition wasn't as stiff as at the big firms.

More important, why do you care about prestige? Your friends like you because you're nice to children and you feed stray cats. People of the opposite sex like you because you can part your hair with your tongue.

(B) THE BIG FIRM

The story at a big firm is somewhat different.

$$

At a big firm, the money is considerable. Sometimes it's astronomical. No one in his right mind would argue that that much money can't make a difference in your life.

You should note, however, that not all the partners at the big firms pull in those six-figure salaries you read about in the *National Inquirer, New York Post,* and *American Lawyer.*

If you picture yourself as Lloyd Cutler when you think about your career in the law, you probably also picture yourself as Caesar when you think about what it must have been like in ancient Rome. But making partner doesn't make you Caesar; it just barely gets you a bleachers seat at the Colosseum.

Job Security

If you make partner at a big firm you'll probably be allowed to stick around for as long as you like. Note, however, that it's a question of being "allowed" to stick around. Allowed by whom? By the partners who run the firm.

But it's a *partnership,* you protest. Doesn't everyone have a vote? Sure, but what you get to vote are your partnership "shares," or "percentage," which are hardly equal from partner to partner. Shares are usually divided up on the basis of seniority, hours worked, and clients brought in.

Seniority is not something you can do anything about. Either you've been there for a long time or you haven't. A lack of seniority isn't necessarily bad: seniority correlates not only with increased partnership shares but also with stodginess, bad teeth, and the wearing of hats.

As for hours worked, most firms will raise your partnership percentage infinitessimally if you work like a slave. (At big firms, the expression is "work like an associate.")

The only path to security and comfort as a partner, even at a large firm, is to have your own client base—to be a "rainmaker."

Scut Work

Being a rainmaker not only increases your job secu-

rity but also frees you from scut work. It frees you from any kind of work. Associates and non-rainmaking partners can take care of *work.*

Won't you at least have to supervise these associates, reviewing and editing the mountains of memoranda they churn out? There's no need. Associates are better at it than you are. All you have to do is sign the documents so your clients will think you still know how to practice law.

Prestige

There's a good bit of prestige connected with partnership in the big firms,* and questioning the destination of the journey may be pointless if you've already arrived. But maybe it's not too late. Try asking yourself what *is* prestige, but high regard in the minds of strangers? And why do you care what strangers think? Have they ever asked what *you* think?

---

* This is true only up to a point. At some of the giant operations the firm letterhead appears to have all the exclusivity of a United Way annual fund roster.

"Maybe my client shot a few people, maybe he didn't . . . but there's a principle at issue here."

"Principles are important to me, too. I do pro bono work for Exxon each month."

"Did I tell you about this dirtball I sent to the Big House last week?"

"Did you see the new Treasury Regs on partnership capital accounts? Fascinating!"

"Hey fella, I'll bet you've got tight briefs."

"They're concise, to be sure, but it's important to make every argument. (Take this brief I filed last week . . .)*

THE AMERICAN BAR ASSOCIATION CONVENTION:

The Public Defender: Former McGovern campaign aide. (Chose N.Y.U. Law school because of its hip clinical program.)* **Motto:** "Society is to blame."

The Rainmaker: Married money. Great B.S. artist, but wouldn't know a limited partnership from a prenuptial agreement. **Motto:** "What me work?"

The Prosecutor: Grew up on tough Chicago's South Side. Lives to put the criminal element behind bars. **Motto:** "Ask for the Chair."

The Tax Lawyer: Passionless eyes. Often forgets to shave. Spends weekends with personal computer. **Motto:** "The Code is Lord."

The Washington Lobbyist: Attended Georgetown night law school. Happy to represent highest bidder for her "contracts." **Motto:** "Make me an offer."

The Corporate Lawyer: Harvard Law Review editor. Young partner at New York megafirm. Had last date two years ago. **Motto:** "Sleep is dispensable."

"Do you think varying levels of culpability can be incorporated into Fourth Amendment doctrine?"

"Sure, it looks like a great job, but believe me, these robes get hot."

"Do you know if any law requires Congressmen to hire only secretaries who can read?"

"I wonder if you could get around Section 16 by transferring stock to your dog and letting it take the short-swing profits . . ."

"I told Redford, 'Rob, Baby, never sign anything without running it by me first.'"

"Let me know if they sue. We'll bury them in enough paper to wipe out a forest of giant redwoods."

A GUIDE TO LEGAL PERSONALITIES

The Professor: Law Review editor-in-chief. Clerked on Supreme Court. Has lectured in same jacket and tie for seven years. **Motto:** "Anything to get published."

The Judge: Appointed to bench after marrying the governor's daughter. Thinks he looks good in basic black; considered ministry for same reason. **Motto:** *"L'état c'est moi."*

The Politico: Voted "Best Dressed Clubbie." Took over Daddy's safe seat in House after graduation. **Motto:** "A reasonable vote for a reasonable price."

The Securities Lawyer: Ex-social worker. Went into law to improve society. Succumbed to lure of big bucks. **Motto:** "Buy low, sell high."

The Entertainment Lawyer: Majored in film and drugs at U.C.L.A. Law. Represents star-studded clientele out of Beverly Hills. **Motto:** "I can relate."

The Litigator: High school debate champion. Voted "Most Narcissistic Senior." **Motto:** "Concede nothing."

THE RAINMAKER

Every lawyer wants to be a rainmaker. Rainmakers run the show.

If the other partners in a law firm don't vote the way the rainmakers want them to vote, on such essential issues as who gets the corner office to whose name goes at the top of the firm letterhead, the rainmakers can walk.*

* "Getting business isn't the most important thing—it's the only thing.... The people who bring in the business are demanding the lion's share of the billings, and if it's not forthcoming, they will take a walk." D. Beckwith, "Inside Washington's Legal Establishment," *The Washingtonian* (April 1983).

"You know, Gottlieb, the law still surges through every inch of my being."

A few rainmakers bring in clients simply by being great lawyers. Take, for example, Joe Flom, New York's tender offer star; Ben White, Atlanta's tax mogul; Mortimer (Bear Tracks) Snerd, Fort Worth's expert on the immigration of Mexican groundhogs.

But most rainmakers get clients through personal connections, and have their work done by senior associates or non-rainmaking partners.

The fact is that if you can bring in clients, you don't need to know a lot of law. You don't need to know how to read. Some rainmakers are dumber than a fundamentalist preacher.

It is not uncommon to hear a non-rainmaking lawyer (or even a drizzler) privately abuse the rainmakers of his firm. In a sneering tone, Partner Attridge might say,

Old Hannaferd hasn't practiced law for years. All he does is show up at noon, take rich clients to lunch at fancy restaurants, and play golf in the afternoon. He isn't a serious lawyer anymore.

All of this is true: rainmakers don't practice law, and they aren't serious lawyers. This is why Partner Attridge hates Old Hannaferd. Old Hannaferd has the job every lawyer dreams of.

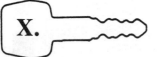

X.

Elements of Style: The Lawyerly Look

There are various points of style every lawyer should observe. For associates, these points can gain you critical mileage in the minds of that vast majority of partners who will never see your work and will know you only socially—or anti-socially, as the case may be. For partners, the idea is essentially the same—there is always someone more senior you need to impress.

(A) DRESS FOR LEGAL SUCCESS

In the world of dress, formality is not synonymous with good taste. Many lawyers bear more than a passing resemblance to Lieutenant Columbo.

By and large this doesn't matter. Lawyers rarely get out of the office, and when they do they usually just see their counterparts at other firms. Still, unless you've already given up hope for a better life, it's worthwhile to pay some attention to how you look.

Males

Conservatism should be your sartorial guide. The rule is: "Think Yiddish, dress British." This doesn't mean you have to be stuffy: your wardrobe of suits can run the gamut from blue to black, with even some festive pin stripes thrown in. The stripes should be narrower than those worn by your former

153

The Diversity Suit.

clients now residing at San Quentin.

Shirts should be white or blue. Shirts with thin pin stripes are okay, but in combination with pin stripe suits and club ties, they clash to produce a Doc Severinsen—style disaster: the "diversity suit."

Always wear a T-shirt under your white shirts. That rug on your chest which dazzles women at the beach each summer looks terrible poking out between your buttons.

Shirts should generally have button-down collars. Non-button-downs are okay as long as they aren't "compass shirts"—the ones with extremely long collars, one of which always sticks out as if it's trying to point north.

Ties should be narrower than the prevailing chic, whatever it is. Buy silk, not burlap. Striped ties or club ties (the ones with the silly looking owls or moose) are best. Never paisley.

Pin-dot ties are okay; large polka dots are not. Especially not those ties with one huge red polka dot that spans the width of the tie and looks like it's still growing— the polka dot that took over St. Louis.

Wear a gold Cross pen in your breast pocket. It is dressy but sufficiently practical to pass muster in the legal context. For actual work, you'll use pencils or those wonderful felt-tip pens that let your thoughts flow like

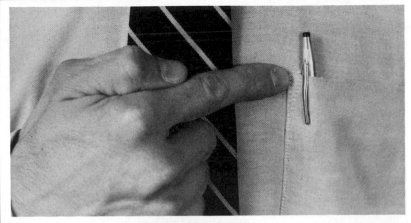

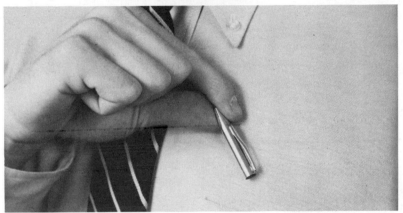

Is it, or isn't it? Oops! Fooled again! When you're wearing this simulated 14 K. gold Cross pen, soon to be marketed by White's Costume Jewelry, Ltd., partners and clients will never suspect that isn't the real thing projecting proudly from your breast pocket, ever ready to execute a multimillion dollar contract. For just $2.69, you can acquire the look of a successful, affluent attorney, even though you can barely cover the installments on your mail-order suit from Hong Kong. Remember: in the law, appearances are everything!

ethnic slurs at a Republican fund raiser, but on those rare occasions when a partner or client turns to you for something with which to sign a brief or contract, you don't want to have to fish through your trouser pockets, only to come up with a tooth-marred Bic with lint balls caught in the clip.

Jewelry is best avoided, particularly gold medallions and big diamond rings that look like what football players get for winning the Super Bowl. The same goes for big watches—you don't need one that tells you the time in Hong Kong and looks like what Lloyd Bridges wore in *Sea Hunt*.

Females

For women, the rules of drabness are comparable; your attire should match your job.

Make-up should be minimized and perfume avoided altogether. You don't want to encourage the senior partner to think of you in the same vein as the women he knew in Paris during the war.

Hemlines should stay below the knees (or partners' hands won't). You should shun dresses with slits up the sides unless (a) you have great legs and (b) you're bucking for a promotion to receptionist.

Your hair style should be inconspicuous, preferably gathered up in a wad in the back. Too many waves and curls will make it look like you take it to Jerome Robbins to be choreographed.

Shoe heels should be low, if not flat. High heels will get you stranded in sub-

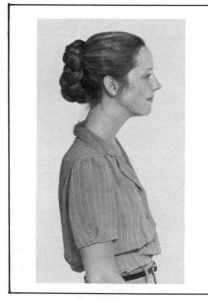

Your coiffure should reflect the preferred legal temperament: uptight! Don't let your hair down—and show the real *you—until after you leave the office.*

way gratings and cause part- ners to confuse you with secretaries.

Large breasts should be avoided. Partners will stare.

(B) BRIEFCASES

Carry a large one. No *business* person would be caught dead carrying a large briefcase—someone *else* handles his grunt work—but lawyers *thrive* on grunt work. Senior partners take pride in walking out of their offices on Friday afternoon with two briefcases, each big enough to hold a human body.

Carrying a large brief- case is part of cultivating the proper image. You needn't have anything in it, although

"It's all over for me . . . Mr. Butterworth found out that the briefcase that I so diligently carry home from the office each night contains my gym clothes."

an article or manuscript is handy in case a senior partner sits so close on the bus one morning that he might notice if you were reading *Sports Illustrated*.

(C) OFFICE PROPS

Subscribe to the *Harvard Law Review*. Other lawyers will rarely remember what law school you went to, and they will *never* remember whether you were on that school's Law Review. If you store your issues on a center shelf of your office (particularly *bound* volumes for the years when you were actually in the YMCA night law program), people will assume you attended Harvard and made Law Review there.

This is a safe trick, because if challenged, you can always claim you're just trying to stay abreast of developments in the law. It is not unduly expensive, because it takes only two year's worth to achieve the desired effect.

This is somewhat akin to hanging a picture of a Su-

REAL LAWYERS EAT
FAST FOOD

A J.D. degree and a passed bar exam do not a *real* lawyer make. There's more to being a *real* lawyer—a lot more.

How can you tell if you're a *real* lawyer, an Arnold Schwarzenegger of a lawyer? Measure yourself by the following criteria:

1. **Real lawyers eat fast food.** The faster the better, and preferably something you can eat at your desk. Eating just gets in the way of work.

2. **Real lawyers don't have tans.** They prefer the library to the beach; it's tough to draft a prospectus lying in the sand.

3. **Real lawyers don't drive flashy cars.** Rainmakers might, but nobody said they're real lawyers. Real lawyers aren't into style and pizzazz.

4. **Real lawyers don't have beards.** Beards are bushy and untidy—they just don't sit right. Even a mustache looks too much like nosehairs grown out of control.

5. **Real lawyers work on Sundays.** *Lots* of lawyers go to the office on Saturdays; that's expected. Only the hard guys can bear it on Sundays, when the ventilation has been off for two days and the air smells so ripe you'd swear it's wearing your old college roommate's gym locker.

6. **Real lawyers don't have erotic daydreams.** They don't have trouble concentrating on their work. To the real lawyer, tax reports are erotic enough to hold their attention.

7. **Real lawyers love to proofread — everything.** Not just legal documents and formal correspondence. Real lawyers proofread street signs, magazine ads, and the little placards under each fish tank at the Boston Aquarium. Nothing makes their day like catching a typo.

8. **Real lawyers don't like children.** Children are noisy, frivolous, distracting. Kids just don't care about the important things in life: class actions, Rule 10b-5, mitigation of damages.

preme Court Justice on your wall to make everyone think you clerked for that Justice. If challenged, you can reply that you happen to admire that Justice a great deal— a reasonable defense unless you've forged on it "To my good friend and able clerk. . . ."

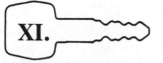

XI.

Alternative Routes: Government Service, Country Law

Private practice in an urban law factory isn't the only route. Some of the finest lawyers around opt for government service. Or head for the hills.

(A) THE GOVERNMENT LAWYER

The primary distinction of government practice is early, hands-on responsibility —none of these two-year warm-up periods before getting to argue a crummy motion for extension of time in a District Court.

A government salary is nothing to write home about, particularly in comparison with what some lawyers make in private practice. But if you measure income in dollars *per hour,* it's far from clear who comes out on top: if private firms spawned the concept of the 25-hour working day, government practice spawned the concept of the 25-hour working week.

Government practice might be right for you—no private firm ever served a bigger client—but don't make any rash decisions. Read the following rules on survival as a government lawyer to make sure you know what you're getting into.

1. **Make sure you have your own desk.** Nothing is certain in government employment. It is too much to hope for a private office, but

demand your own desk. In fact, negotiate this before you accept the job.

2. **Hone your secretarial skills.** If you got through law school without knowing how to type, now is the time to learn.

Some good news and some bad news. The good news is that word processing machines and related equipment are not beyond the technical competence of a highly trained professional like yourself. The bad news is that there is a reason they're so simple. Read on.

There are a number of fine secretaries in the government (people debate whether the number is three or four), but you will not get one right off the bat, say, within your first decade. You will get another kind, to whom filing her fingernails is more important than filing your briefs.

Do not be too harsh in judging these secretaries. They work under trying conditions—handling five lawyers' briefs and correspondence between 10:00 A.M. and 3:30 P.M., with two hours out for lunch, "All My Children," and "The Young and The Restless." * In judging them, consider that *your* output would suffer if you wore Sony Walk-Man earphones all day.

Secretarial self-reliance is essential to survival in government practice. You don't have to be able to take apart and reassemble a Xerox 2000-X copier—but it wouldn't hurt. You will invariably be the next person to use a machine after someone has dropped a box of paper clips into its guts. NOTE: when the lights start blinking, do not panic—leave quietly and find another machine.

3. **Dress functionally.** Dress is not as important in the government as in private practice. A government salary can't support a fancy wardrobe, and let's face it, who wants to sit behind a metal desk wearing a $300 suit?

4. **Avoid drift.** The pace of government practice can

---

* These strains can result in unconscious editorial contributions to your work product. A lawyer who dictated the words "Refer the matter to the Criminal Division" got back for his signature a neatly typed letter reading "Refer the mother to the Criminal Division." Always proofread your work.

GOVERNMENT TRAVEL

If the government has billions to spend on MX missiles, a lot of that comes from what it *doesn't* spend on its legal staff. A military force equipped as poorly as the average government legal division couldn't mount a successful panty raid on a girl's prep school.

The government's miserly policies toward its own are most apparent when it comes to travel. Government lawyers travel a good bit. The big guns in Washington don't feel comfortable leaving important cases to the local crew in places like Iowa. Can you blame them?

The government lawyer who has to fly somewhere is usually surprised to learn that there is a class lower than coach—and he may be in trouble if he's allergic to animals. Also, the government would prefer that he kill two days city-hopping between Washington and St. Louis rather than spend an extra $40.00 for a direct flight. Given the tightwad government per diem, it would be cheaper even if it took a week.

The government lawyer on the road doesn't have a wide array of hotel options. If he's not crashing on a friend's sofa, he's staying at one of the orange-roofed "Johnson" establishments. While his counterparts in private practice are limousining around town in search of haute cuisine on which to squander client funds, the government lawyer considers himself lucky to find an all-beef patty within walking distance of his room.

be casual and pleasant, to say the least. You will undoubtedly be tempted, on a prolonged basis, to relax, settle back, borrow your secretary's Sony Walkman and give no thought to the future. Resist this temptation!

You're there to learn and advance, not drift. Government practice has a thousand dead ends—*somebody* has to write those regulations governing the labelling of cherry pits—and you don't want to find yourself stranded.

Cherry regulations—drafting these could be the end of the line.

Don't assume it will be obvious when your career development in the government has come to a halt. Unlike the private sector, the government doesn't operate on an up-or-out system. You might be doing the same thing in 30 years that you did when you began. (If you doubt this will impair your mental acuity, try talking with the demented "lifer" at the end of the hall.)

At a minimum, learn skills that are transferable to the private sector, *e.g.,* litigation or securities. Reviewing documents under the Freedom of Information Act might seem interesting for two days, maybe three—but a year of it could turn you into a government lawyer forever.

(B) THE COUNTRY LAWYER

The joy of being a country lawyer, like that of being a country doctor, is that you're also part psychologist, part family counsellor, and maybe part plumber and animal midwife.

The *problem* with being a country lawyer is that you have to *live* in the country, which requires learning to whittle, chew tobacco, and spit. Otherwise, people won't cotton to you.

Depending on your tastes, country life might not be so bad. Think of baseball players—they *love* chewing tobacco, and for their salaries there's nothing you wouldn't chew. You might not get off on the sight of your partner making functional use of the spittoon at the foot of his desk every fifteen minutes, but who's to say that's worse than being told to perform anatomically impossible acts on yourself in a New York subway each morning. (If the mugger is armed, you may find the acts aren't impossible.)

The major difference between the practice of a big city lawyer and that of a country or even suburban lawyer is the level of perfection that goes into the work. Big city lawyers do a perfect job on every project, no matter how disproportionate the costs of a perfect job are to the stakes involved. They'll not only produce an 80-page lease for a one room apartment, but also spend thousands of dollars proofreading the 80-page lease.

Country and suburban lawyers can't do this. Their clients are individuals or small companies (Tuscaloosa Sorghum & Grits, Inc.) who just can't afford it. For this reason country and suburban lawyers have to do something that big city lawyers never do: they have to pull in the reins, perform cost-benefit analysis, exercise *judgment*.

NOTE: It's easy to *become* a country lawyer. Just drive into the country and hang up a shingle: "Suits pressed." However, if you're planning to become a country lawyer in the South, your first priority should be to buy a King James version of the Bible, and master the use of words like "thence," "forsook," and "begat." After Sam Ervin's performance in the Senate Watergate hearings, it's expected—no less than being able to put down a whole plateful of collards and opossum with a smile.

Sam Ervin, Jr., Country Lawyer. Encyclopedic knowledge of Holy Scriptures.

XII

Women and the Law
(YOU DON'T HAVE TO WEAR BRIEFS TO WRITE THEM)

Most law school classes these days are one-third to one-half female. Even the most progressive of the large law firms, however, can boast only a handful of

"So you went to law school and now you want to practice law . . . I think that's cute."

169

female partners. It seems they'd prefer to keep the partnership an all-male club —and hold partners' meetings in a locker room, where they could talk dirty and pop each other with rolled-up towels.

This will change over time. As women one-by-one make partner, they'll exert a beneficially inhibiting influence. At partnership elections, old codgers will feel increasingly reluctant to raise the issue of the size of female associates' breasts.

Let there be no doubt: lawyers still have a ways to go. They have never been as bad, however, as construction workers, sailors, or stock brokers.

This is partly because lawyers are too tired and overworked to maintain a standard level of interest in sex. Like prisoners of war, whose libidinal urges take a back seat to the demands of survival, lawyers repress their basic impulses in the interests of by-laws, trust indentures, and promissory notes.

In certain New York corporate takeover firms, Dolly Parton could walk the hallways without raising an eyebrow.

Some partners do find the time and energy to nurture their skepticism about women as lawyers. They ask, "If women are so equal, why is Bella Abzug so short?" These guys have serious differences with the twentieth century.

There are several strategies women can adopt in response. (*See* SIDEBAR, p. 172). But what is required more than any strategy or program of change is time. Women are getting into the top law schools and excelling.* They're getting into the top law firms and continuing to excel. Sandy O'Connor didn't get onto the Supreme Court because she was fooling around with Ed Meese.

Perhaps more important, women in business schools are excelling. Over time these women will run the companies that will become the clients of women in the law. When women become rain-

*Fewer than 2,200 women, or 4 percent of the total law school population, were enrolled in accredited law schools in 1964. A decade later, the number had increased to 21,788, or 21 percent. In 1981 it had reached 44,986, or 35 percent of the total law school population.

makers, their success is as-
sured. At that point the only
question is whether women
will start talking dirty and
popping each other with
rolled-up towels.

Justice Sandra Day O'Connor.

HOW IS A WOMAN TO COPE?

In any law firm with partners old enough to have gray hair (or no hair), a woman will encounter "traditional" attitudes. There are three alternative strategies she can adopt in response.

1. *The Crusader.* This bold approach involves pointing out every indiscretion and protesting every inequity, no matter how minor the offense or how senior the offending partner. "*You* get out of the elevator first, hairbag!" It's a noble battle, but exhausting and potentially fatal to one's career. Make sure you know what you're getting into.

2. *The Mata Hari.* A few women, motivated by contempt or frustration, attempt to exploit those feminine resources that male partners appear most willing to recognize and reward. You can spot a hard-core Mata Hari by her black mesh stockings with seams.

The Mata Hari. *A dazzling effect, but will the court pay attention to your arguments?*

3. *The Survivor.* This pragmatic approach consists of equal parts diplomacy, competence, thick skin, and a strong sense of humor. "Sure, I'll get you some coffee, Mr. Turk—if you'll pick up some pantyhose for me when you go out to lunch." It includes traces of Katharine Hepburn-like insouciance and

Margaret Mead-like tolerance of neanderthals.

This approach may involve a few concessions to circumstance. But these concessions are purely cosmetic. In legal jargon, they are procedural rather than substantive. You should not feel your core values threatened in situations that require you to endure a conversation about sports, or to resist running around the room with an air freshener when someone lights up a cigar.

"Frankly, we waited so long to hire our token female because we wanted to be damn certain it wasn't just a fad."

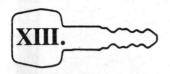

XIII

Legal Writing

("EXCUSE ME, BUT . . . WHAT DOES THIS SAY IN ENGLISH?")

Everyone knows that legal writing is different from regular writing. People can understand regular writing.

Legal writing is instantly recognizable. There's no mistaking a "forthwith" or a "hereinafter." You can spot a "party of the first part" a mile away.

Why do lawyers write that way?

First, they like big words. *Everybody* likes big words, but drafting briefs and contracts all day lets you get good at it.

A lawyer will say "automobile" when he could say "car," and he'll say "mass transportation vehicle" when he could say "bus." He'll even say "practicable" when he means "practical." No one outside the law has ever heard of the word "practicable."

The second trait that makes lawyers write so peculiarly is that they are meticulous by nature. This translates not only into aberrant eating habits,* but also into exceedingly precise prose.

Take the following sentence that might appear in a brief relating to a "morals" prosecution:

> "Instead of building an ordinary hotel, the Board of Trustees decided to set up a brothel, which is the subject of the present action."

This sentence would distress most lawyers, not be-

---

* Watch how some corporate and tax attorneys eat all of each food on their plates before moving to the next food, instead of moving back and forth between them as normal people do.

175

cause a sober person couldn't follow it, but because of the pronoun "which" (in the fifth line).

The average lawyer would fear that a reader might be confused: does "which" refer to the brothel? To the Board of Trustees? To the decision to go for the brothel over the hotel? To the morality of it all?

This mere hint of a possibility of confusion would torture the lawyer's conscience. The same craving for order that led him to color-code his notes in law school would lead him to re-write the above sentence as follows:

> "Instead of building an ordinary hotel, the Board of Trustees decided to set up a brothel, which *brothel* is the subject of the present action."

The additional word adds nothing but length to this sentence. It distracts the reader by its unnatural placement.

But a lawyer would always say *which brothel*, just as he would always say *which contract, which court,* or *which* anything else he could think of. The extra word satisfies his infancy based urge to keep things tidy. With it he'll sleep easier tonight, gurgling and cooing, at peace with the world.

The third trait that accounts for lawyers' bizarre writing style is innate conservatism.

The average lawyer is not bold by nature. His ambition is to go through life with his ass fully covered. To this end he qualifies everything he writes, instinctively fearful of being caught in a lie, or even a metaphor.

The lawyer will tell you it's his *client* he's trying to protect, or that he's just trying to preserve his credibility in the eyes of the judge. This is about as accurate as the claim that he's wearing a vest to keep warm.

* * *

These peculiar tendencies are most evident in partners editing the work of associates. Every partner fancies himself a grammarian. He would edit Strunk and White. There is no sentence so straightforward and simple that he will not happily torture it beyond recognition.

Take the sentence "The sky is blue."

No junior associate would be so naive as to think this proposition could pass muster in a big firm. If he made it through law school, he knows enough to say, "The sky is *generally* blue."

Better yet, "The sky generally *appears* blue."

For extra syllables, "The sky generally appears *to be* blue."

A senior associate seeing this sentence might take pity on the junior associate and explain that before showing it to a partner the junior associate should put it in a more "lawyerly" form. At the very least the sentence should be revised to say, "In some parts of the world, what is generally thought of as the sky sometimes appears to be blue."

Armed with these qualifiers, the junior associate thinks himself protected.

His conversation with the reviewing partner will proceed thus:

Partner Carter:

"You say here that in some parts of the world, what is generally thought of as the sky sometimes appears to be blue. I assume this is just an early draft. Could I see the final version?"

Associate Williams:

"Uh, that's all I have right now . . . what exactly do you mean?"

Partner Carter:

"Well, it's a bit bald, don't you think? I mean, just to come right out and assert it as fact."

Associate Williams:

"I beg your pardon? Are we talking about the same thing?"

Partner Carter:

"Well, this business about 'the sky'—what did you mean by 'the sky'?"

Associate Williams:

"Well, I meant what I see when I look up . . . at least, when I'm outside. Isn't that what everyone sees?"

Partner Carter:

"Okay, if you mean *only* when you're outside, you have to say so. Our opponents in this case would love to rip us apart on that kind of error. And what about at night? Even at night? I see stars at night— are they blue? Do you mean everything *but* stars, or do you mean when there are no stars out?"

Associate Williams:

"I meant during the day, I guess."

Partner Carter:

"You *guess*. Williams, this is serious business. We can't go around guessing at things. Besides, what about the sun? If it's daytime, the sun will be out—or do you know something I don't?"

Associate Williams:

"Well, sure . . . I mean, no, I don't. . . . But no one in his right mind looks at the sun. You'd go blind."

Partner Carter:

"What support do you have for this comment about 'some parts of the world'? *Which* parts? Do we need to state it so broadly? Can't we just say 'in Cleveland' or wherever we mean?"

Associate Williams:

"That sounds fine to me. I just never thought anyone would challenge . . . that is, who would disagree with . . ."

Partner Carter:

"And what do you mean by 'generally thought of'?

"SPEAKING AS A LAWYER . . ."

Lawyers commonly preface their remarks with "Speaking as a lawyer. . . ." Is this a boast? A disclaimer?

Whatever else it is, it's unnecessary. It's *obvious* when someone is "speaking as a lawyer."

For one thing, lawyers over-enunciate their words, smacking their lips and pronouncing each syllable crisply and distinctly, as if talking to someone for whom English isn't a native tongue.

This can be irritating. Sometimes it makes you want to insert their tongues into the office paper shredder.

Lawyers also talk in uncommonly full, formal sentences. They take pains to select just the right words for their fine thoughts, with mid-sentence pauses so long you could squeeze in a reading of *War and Peace*.

It's as if they're talking on the record, for posterity. A lot posterity cares.

Thought of by whom? Lawyers? Scientists? Morticians? Dammit, Williams, this piece has more holes in it than Swiss cheese. I haven't seen such sloppiness in all my years at Cavil, Quibble & Quiver. Take it back and see if you can't do a little better this time around."

Even more startling for new associates than this distortion of English by verbally incontinent old timers is the *process* by which legal briefs are written.

Law students are taught that judges decide cases on the basis of previous cases, that the system is ruled by precedent. Accordingly, they assume that the way lawyers write briefs is by researching previous cases and constructing arguments based on those cards.

What *really* happens is that partners or senior asso-

PRINCIPLES OF LEGAL WRITING

1. Never use one word where ten will do.

2. Never use a small word where a big one will do suffice.

3. Never use a simple statement where it appears that one of substantially greater complexity will achieve comparable goals.

4. Never use English where Latin, *mutatis mutandis*, will do.

5. Qualify virtually everything.

6. Do not be embarrassed about repeating yourself. Do not be embarrassed about repeating yourself.

7. Worry about the difference between "which" and "that."

8. In pleadings and briefs, that which is defensible should be stated. That which is indefensible, but which you wish were true, should merely be suggested.

9. Never refer to your opponent's "arguments"; he only makes "assertions," and his assertions are always "bald."

10. If a layman can read a document from beginning to end without falling asleep, it needs work.

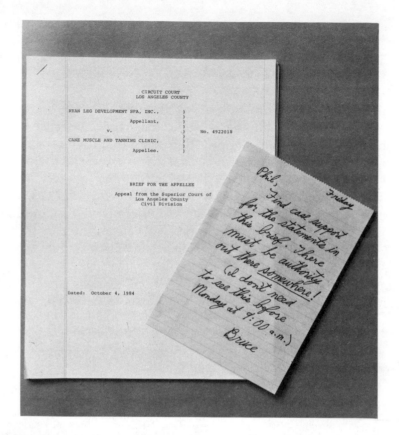

ciates write the briefs *first*. They know what they want to say; they know how their argument has to come out.

Then they turn the brief over to a junior associate, with each assertion followed by a bracketed note: "[Find case support for this statement.]" *

---

* Every firm's history includes at least one story of a new recruit fired for failing to catch all of these open references in the final brief. Judges tend to get upset when they find remarks like "[There must be authority for this *somewhere*]" or "[Cite usual crap]."

This process obviously assumes that there is case support for anything. There is.

What about those few propositions so well hidden that they cannot be located even by the army of associates that big firms will readily commit to the search?

You do with these propositions what Thomas Jefferson did with the proposition "all men are created equal": you put them up front and call them "self-evident."

"Cogswell, find me legal authority for the proposition that 'the law is an ass.' "

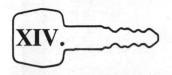

XIV.

Drafting Legal Documents: Contracts, Leases, Wills
(MORE IS BETTER . . . UNTIL IT BEGINS TO MAKE SENSE)

"**L**egal writing" is different from "legal drafting." Lawyers use the former term to refer to briefs, letters and memoranda, but they like to say they "draft" contracts, leases and wills. "Draft" suggests refined skills, even artistic capabilities.

Drafting truly impenetrable documents is not easy. Many young lawyers' initial attempts at legal drafting are rejected outright, with senior partners offering such helpful comments as "This won't do. I can still get the gist of some of the sentences."

Fortunately for young lawyers, most kinds of documents that lawyers have to draft have been drafted hundreds of times before. The large law firms have countless file drawers full of old documents, and the associate who is asked to draft, say, an industrial revenue bond, needs merely to rummage through the files for an old one that looks about right.

A paralegal could do it. Paralegals *do* do it.

Solo practitioners and lawyers in small firms don't have it much harder. There are hundreds of commercially sold "mumbo-jumbo books," with model contracts, leases and wills of every sort imaginable.

If your client is a Hindu who wants to leave all his worldly possessions to his sacred cow, the mumbo-jumbo books have several versions of the form you need. Just fill in the name and address of the cow.

TYPES OF LEGAL DOCUMENTS

It's bad enough that legal documents are about as short and easy to carry around as a complete set of the Encyclopaedia Britannica, but why must they also come in so many different types?

Fundamentally, there are only four types of legal documents:

1. boring;
2. extremely boring;
3. comatose;
4. pull-the-plug-and-let-me-die-with-dignity.

There are four types of lawyers who produce these documents:

1. boring;
2. extremely boring;
3. comatose;
4. those for whom the plug has been pulled. (The last are easy to spot —they're the ones with dignity.)

Notwithstanding this simplicity at one level, legal documents come in a dazzling array. Whether you need something to paper over a deal or, more important, to put under the short leg of your dining-room table, you have an impressive smorgasbord to choose from.

In part this reflects the complexity of modern business transactions, in part lawyers' zeal for their trade. It also reflects the rabbit-like procreative powers of legal documents: left alone in a drawer at night, leases beget subleases, wills beget trusts, deeds beget mortgages, debentures beget subordinated convertibles. Thus far the only known form of birth control is a client who refuses to pay his legal bill —revealing in yet another field the prophylactic power of a firm "No!"

HOW TO DRAFT A CONTRACT FROM SCRATCH

Legal writing requires a great deal of skill on those rare occasions when the client wants to do something that has never been done before. Then you can't rely on old forms; you have to obfuscate on your own.

In such situations you should proceed thus:.

First, describe in normal language whatever it is the client wants to do. Then lengthen it.

A good way to begin the lengthening process is to make express provision for every conceivable turn of events, no matter how remote. Be sure to describe which party to the contract is at risk if an outbreak of malaria among Indonesian cane harvesters jeopardizes the Kentucky market for thoroughbred foals, particularly if the contract deals with office space in Seattle.

Continue the lengthening process by qualifying the irrelevant and defining the obvious.

With regard to definitions, do not hesitate to define things in improbable ways. A good lawyer feels no compunction about defining "person" to mean "corporations, partnerships, and livestock"; "automobile" to mean "airplanes, submarines, and bicycles"; and

"I tell you, Galworthy, it's the height of the art . . . a document composed one hundred percent of fine print and disclaimers."

AMONG v. BETWEEN

A lawyer who doesn't know the difference between "among" and "between" has missed his true calling as a bricklayer.

When the parties to a contract number three or more, the contract should recite that it is entered "by and *among*" the parties. When the parties number fewer than three (usually two), the contract should recite that it is entered "by and *between*" the parties when they number two. Why it is not enough to say simply that the contract is entered "by" the parties is an issue going to the very heart of the law.

"cash" to mean "stocks, bonds, and whiskey."

Do not stop with hundreds of useless definitions and qualifications. Go through it again and again, expanding clauses and inserting redundancies. This will enable you to avoid the perils of certain forms of punctuation—such as the period.

Once you have revised your original description to the point that no one without a Ph.D. in semantics could understand it, the next step is to break it down into numerous paragraphs, sub-paragraphs, sub-sub-paragraphs, *ad infinitum*. This way the various units can refer back and forth to each other ("as provided herinabove in Subsection 43(d)(1)(A)(viii), except for sub-part Q/3-a thereof . . ."), thus eliminating any hint of continuity or readability.

By the time you've completed these steps, your contract should defy analysis by Japanese cryptologists. All that remains is to add a few exhibits, attachments, and appendices. These don't have to be relevant to anything. They're for bulk. The height of the art is to have an attachment to an exhibit to an appendix, with cross-references to other documents not even included.

LEGAL MACHISMO: THE RUNNING OF THE PEN AT PAMPLONA

Lawyers say words are their "stock in trade." If so,

DRAFTING AND PUNCTUATION: THE PERILS OF PERIODS

A period marks the end of a sentence. This is clearly understood. For this reason periods should be avoided. Commas, too, tend to clarify rather than obfuscate.

But the indeterminacy of colons and semicolons lets them mean anything you want them to mean (which is not to say you have to let the reader in on your secret). With colons and semicolons, sentences can be extended indefinitely; subjects can be separated from predicates by pages numbering in the double figures.

Dashes and parentheticals, if properly employed, can yield a nicely convoluted sentence. But God only knows the proper use and meaning of a colon. And a semicolon is just half of that.

Far more important than anything you *say* in a document is whether you are consistent in your use of letters, numbers, and Roman numerals. The same lawyers and judges who view a readable contract as beneath contempt become distraught upon encountering a bungled cross-reference forward or backward.

Revising documents is therefore fraught with danger. If you eliminate —or, more likely, add—a single clause or paragraph early on, all subsequent numbers and letters are thrown out of kilter.

This is why you see so many amendments and addenda located at the *end* of legal documents. Lawyers are mortally afraid of screwing up the numbers.

I(a)(1)(A)(i)(aa)
II(b)(2)(B)(ii)(bb)
III(c)(3)(C)(iii)(cc)

they are burdened by an excess of inventory.

Why are lawyers enamored of length in their documents? Why do they get off on sheer bulk? There's a touch of Hemingway in everyone. But lawyers can't

THE MYTH OF THE REASONABLE CONTRACT

Contracts, leases and the like are not neutral documents. Lawyers draft them for specific clients, and their terms invariably favor the client of the lawyer who drafted them.

A lease drafted by a landlord's lawyer, for example, will provide for late fees if the tenant doesn't pay his rent on time, and capital punishment if it happens twice. The same lease drafted by a tenant's lawyer will give the tenant a 20-day grace period for tardy payments and provide for apologies by the tenant if he doesn't pay by then.

So one-sided are most documents that lawyers' form files contain two versions of each type, one version drafted for one side, one for the other. The lawyers could just as easily swap sides and use the other forms in their files.

What goes on in contract negotiations is the lawyers sit around identifying the outrageous provisions in each others' drafts—ultimately producing a reasonable document. The virtue of this process is that it enables each side's lawyer to drive a "hard bargain" —and generate enormous fees.

run with the bulls or go deep-sea fishing, so they find surrogate manhood in their papers. They deny the desk-bound tameness of their lives by conceiving of their documents as weapons of battle.

A lawyer refers to a contract of which he is particularly proud as "bulletproof," meaning it can hold up even under close judicial scrutiny. He speaks of "hammering" his opponents with a forceful brief, or "nailing them to the wall'' with a fiercely worded motion.

This button-down, white collar brand of cojones finds its most comical expression in the pride lawyers take in the length of their documents. A lawyer will boast of a 280-page contract the way a sportsman boasts of a 300-pound fish. He'll show a 200-page brief to his family and friends like a little boy showing off the hole he dug in the backyard.

The difference is that the 300-pound fish and the hole in the backyard didn't cost anyone thousands of dollars.

Also, if you thought about it for a long time, you could probably find something socially useful about the hole and the fish.

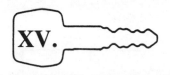

XV

Lawyers and Humor

(THERE ARE NO FUNNY LAWYERS— ONLY FUNNY PEOPLE WHO MADE CAREER MISTAKES)

When big firm corporate lawyers claim to act on behalf of "the public interest," you have to wonder who's writing their material. These are funny guys!

Lawyers are not known for their scintillating wit, however. They are perceived as dour, humorless, and sober—and for this reason are often mistaken for Baptists.

The perception of lawyers as humorless is not entirely their fault. It is partly because the occasions on which people consult their lawyers are serious. People involved in divorce proceedings show marginal appreciation for even the finest wit. Deceased relatives, automobile decapitations, and income tax returns provoke limited mirth.

Moreover, who can be humorous when he's exhausted and fully prepared to do a face-down in his dinner? A lawyer at the end of the week is like a marathoner on his 26th mile—he's tired and smells bad.

The fact that lawyers are not the *source* of much humor in the world does not mean they cannot enjoy a good joke told by someone else. Lawyers laugh long and hard at jokes told by judges, wealthy clients, and Internal Revenue Service examiners. Lawyers may not *know* many jokes, but they are able to *appreciate* jokes—with respect to any subject except themselves.

191

When judges joke, lawyers laugh.

Actually, associates in large law firms are no more humorless than the public at large. Given the comical nature of most of what such associates do (and all of what they bill), it is surprising that more professional comedians do not emerge from their ranks. Charging $120 per hour for proofreading documents breeds an acute sense of the absurd.

The most peculiar aspect of humor in the life of associates is the extent to which they must confine it to other associates. Partners who have been known to laugh— *out loud*—in response to jokes told by other partners show a remarkable reluctance to acknowledge humor out of the mouths of associates.

This behavior could reflect a conscious effort to impress young lawyers with the seriousness of the firm's work. It could also reflect partners' revulsion at the thought of how associates spend their time—not an unreasonable response.

Most likely it reflects a psychological defense mechanism. Partners don't want to grow too intimate with people who (by all odds) will be compelled to leave the firm after expending their finest energies. This phenomenon resembles the reluctance felt by jailers in ancient Rome to become familiar with prisoners about to face the lions.

* * *

Legal Graffiti

There once was a man
  named Rex,
Whose "thing" was too
  small for his sex.
When he was booked for
  exposure
The judge said, on dis-
  closure:
*"De minimis non curat
  lex."* *

* The law does not care about small matters.

A TRUE STORY

One day, while crossing the street, a young lawyer was struck by a bus. He died and went to Heaven, where he was cordially greeted by God.

God said, "Welcome! You must be ready for a rest. Not many people live to be your age."

"What do you mean?" the lawyer said. "I'm only 37."

"You must be misremembering," said God. "According to your time sheets, you're 142 years old."

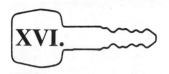

XVI

The Courts

(OLD LITIGATORS NEVER DIE: THEY JUST LOSE THEIR APPEAL)

Litigators are procedural-ists. They care less about who gets beheaded than about whether the guillotine is well oiled and running smoothly.

"Would Your Honor please instruct the witness just to answer the question."

195

When a litigator receives a Complaint charging his client with sawing the beaks off someone's prize pelicans, he doesn't call his client and say, "My God, Steve, that's disgusting. Is any of it true?" Instead he goes over the Complaint with a fine-tooth comb, asking questions like:

> "When was this Complaint filed? Maybe the statute of limitations has run out."

> or

> "Did the plaintiff state where the alleged sawing occurred? Maybe we could knock the suit out for filing in the wrong jurisdiction, or for insufficient specificity of charges."

Obviously, none of these questions has anything to do with justice and fairness. But to the litigator, they're an essential part of the system.

What system? The so-called "adversary system," which rests on the curious premise that out of the clash of lies, truth will emerge.

The basic problem with this system is that neither party has an interest in reaching a result that's fair for both sides. Each side goes for *all* the marbles, not just half. Each side obscures and obstructs as much as possible.

The litigator's role in this system is to help his client obscure and obstruct. In "discovery," for example, when each side gets to ask the other side for information, does either lawyer turn to his client and say, "Give him the papers, Jake. We have nothing to hide."? Of course not. The lawyers procrastinate for months, ultimately disclosing the minimum amount possible, or burying the truth in a mountain of irrelevancies. Both sides' lawyers then go back and forth to the judge, filing "Motions To Compel Disclosure." The process takes years—and generates gigantic legal fees.

The amazing thing is that litigators are unembarrassed by their role. They like it. When they describe themselves as "hired guns," they do so *with pride!*

Needless to say, a litigator shouldn't be someone who embarrasses easily or thinks a lot about the end result of his life's labors. However, a lot of young lawyers get sucked into litigation because that's all law school has really taught them to do. Sadly, a number of perfectly nice people, fully capable of being embarrassed, end up as litigators.

"He always enjoyed playing devil's advocate."

LITIGATION POSTURING

Litigation is a form of low theater. Lawyers are constantly posturing, manifesting in their papers and in the courtroom passions that as lawyers they are incapable of feeling but that are calculated to enlist the support of the judge or jury.

Occasionally lawyers on opposing sides of a case actually hate each other, either because their fees hang in the balance, because they have convinced themselves that they genuinely feel the passions they pretend, or because they're inherently odious.

By and large, however, their passions are totally contrived.

Set forth below is a list of the eight most common litigation poses.

1. **Righteous indignation.** The lawyer's goal in adopting this pose is to suggest that his opponent's case is not only wrong on the law but also ethically questionable. Lawyers usually adopt this pose when there is no law on their side.

2. **Moral outrage.** This is like righteous indignation, only stronger. It is the pose of a divorce lawyer defending a physician who has abandoned his 50-year-old wife for his 25-year-old nurse, and wonders why he should have to give up any of his hard-earned money to support his four kids by his first wife.

3. **Disdain.** This pose is commonly adopted by large firms defending wealthy corporations against one another. The idea is to convince the judge that the other firm has descended to the level of a dirtball ambulance chaser trying to squeeze a few bucks out of the first firm's successful but socially responsible client (who didn't *mean* to pour radioactive waste into the municipal reservoir).

4. **Intimacy.** This is the pose of well-known lawyers battling obscure plaintiffs represented by obscure solo practitioners. Hotshot lawyers use this pose, augmented with winks and hints of levity, to establish a personal relationship with

"Terrible day in court . . . I exhibited moral outrage when I meant to show righteous indignation."

the judge, suggesting without stating that *good* lawyers ("like you and me, Judge") can see that the plaintiff is a few pickles short of the barrel.

5. **Persecuted.** This pose is frequently utilized by civil rights lawyers representing minority defendants in cases brought by the federal government. It can be particularly advantageous where pre-trial questioning establishes that the jurors feel strong messianic impulses and voted for George McGovern.

6. **Bewildered.** This is the pose of the lawyer whose opponents have just scored a direct hit, who have made a telling argument to which he has no reply. He resorts to this pose in a last-ditch effort to suggest that their argument makes no sense and is irrelevant to

the facts of the case.

7. **Earnest.** This would-I-lie-to-you? pose is employed by lawyers with particularly guilty-looking clients—such as Roman Polanski on a morals charge, or a professional athlete charged with possession of cocaine.

8. **Disappointed.** With this pose a lawyer attempts to suggest that the devastating points just scored by his opponents are, to his sadness, underhanded and deceitful. Often the lawyer will season this pose with a pinch of parental solicitude, as if for a child gone astray. This is the pose of a lawyer who sees his client about to go to jail and his fee about to go out the window.

SPECIALTY COURTS
(Have I got a court for you . . .)

States have, in addition to the usual hierarchy of courts, a variety of specialized courts that dispense factory line, bulk process justice. You're bound to be dragged into one of these sooner or later, so it's good to know what they do.

Probate Courts. These courts resolve disputes over the property of dead people. If someone dies owning enough money for round trip cab fare to the Probate Court, people will fight over it.

Family Courts. As every divorced person knows, you have to get permission to get divorced. Family courts are where you go to request such permission—a degrading experience similar to having to raise your hand during an exam to request permission to go to the bathroom.

Landlord - Tenant Courts. These courts decide whether a landlord *really* has to provide heat and hot water, and whether a tenant *really* has to pay his rent. Landlord-tenant conflicts tend to evoke judges' latent class-based political sentiments. Hence tenants should be wary of judges wearing expensive cuff links. Landlords should avoid judges with beards.

Juvenile Courts. As Art Linkletter knew, kids do

the darnedest things. Some of them break windows, steal cars, and stick sharp objects into people they don't know. Juvenile courts decide whether these high-spirited youngsters should lose their allowances for a period or whether less severe discipline will suffice.

Small Claims Courts. These courts decide disputes over sums up to, say, $700. Hence the nickname "small change court."

YOU AND "THE COURT"
(Ten commandments of courtroom demeanor)

1. The Judge is always "Your Honor" or "The Court."

2. The Judge's clerk is always "Your Honor" or "The Court."

3. The Judge's prior ruling is never "mistaken," although frequently it is "inapplicable to the facts of the present case."

4. The Judge is never "late," although frequently the press of business interrupts his schedule.

5. The Judge is always to be thanked for his thoughtful ruling, even if he has just sentenced your client to life.

6. The Judge has never "forgotten" anything, although frequently you must "refresh the Court's recollection" of key facts.

7. The Judge has always "read the papers," but frequently you must "draw the Court's attention" to key points therein.

8. The Judge knows every relevant statute and case, so you must introduce points of law with "As the Court knows...."

9. The Judge will never "wait a minute" or "hold on," but you may "beg the Court's pardon" or "pray for the Court's momentary indulgence."

10. The Judge never has to "go to the bathroom," but sometimes "the Court will take a brief recess."

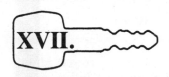

XVII.

Legal Ethics
(AND OTHER GREAT OXYMORONS)

The very concept of legal ethics triggers guffaws within the general populace. It is viewed by most as a contradiction in terms, an "oxymoron" along the lines of "postal service," "military intelligence," "scholar-athlete," and "Justice Rehnquist."

Lawyers profess to take legal ethics very seriously. It is a required part of law school curricula. It is covered on the bar exam in every state.*

As an academic matter, legal ethics is no worse than Kant's *Groundwork of the Metaphysics of Morals* as a cure for insomnia.

As a practical matter, however, law students pay marginal attention to this subject. The course on legal ethics usually consists of a short seminar at which attendance plummets as soon as the word spreads that it will be graded Pass/Fail. (Students have been known to depart in mid-lecture upon receiving this message.)

Moreover, any hypothetical problem encountered on a law school final or even on a bar exam can always be answered, "It's a tough case, but I would never do it myself."

Notwithstanding its irrelevance to current legal practice, legal ethics receives lip service from judges, law professors and bar organizations. Hence every lawyer should have a passing familiarity with the Code of Professional Responsibility.

The Code consists of

---

* Our survey of state bar exams was not comprehensive. No one in New Jersey was willing to comment on legal ethics.

seven broad Canons. (The high-mindedness of its drafters is reflected in their use of the word "Canon"—which smacks of papal authority and reflects the judicial urge to exercise divine power.) Each Canon is backed up by several Ethical Considerations and nuts-and-bolts Disciplinary Rules. These are discussed briefly below:

Canon 1. A Lawyer Should Assist in Maintaining the Integrity and Competence of the Profession.

Of course. And grass is green, the sky is blue, and vomit is disgusting.

Canon 2. A Lawyer Should Assist the Legal Profession in Fulfilling Its Duty To Make Legal Counsel Available.

The idea here is that lawyers have an obligation to see to it that poor people and unpopular people (and even poor, unpopular people) should be able to get a lawyer when they need one. Many corporate lawyers feel that they fulfill this obligation by answering tax questions for the local Republican Club.

Canon 3. A Lawyer Should Assist in Preventing the Unauthorized Practice of Law.

Ostensibly directed to protecting lay people from charlatans, this rule rests on the same foundation as the exorbitant fees required for admission to the bar: an unembarrassed desire to limit competition. Ethical Consideration 3-7, which accompanies this Canon, mandates that a lawyer "should not . . . share legal fees with a layman." It is unclear why the drafters of this rule were worried about lawyers sharing their legal fees with anyone.

Canon 4. A Lawyer Should Preserve the Confidences and Secrets of a Client.

The Canon embodies the so-called "attorney-client privilege," akin to the priest-penitent privilege and the doctor-patient privilege. But note one exception to this Canon. Disciplinary Rule 4-101(C) (4) authorizes a lawyer to reveal whatever confidences are "necessary to establish or collect his fee." Principles are principles, but hey, there's no need to let things get out of hand.

Canon 5. A Lawyer Should Exercise Independent Judgment on Behalf of a Client.

What this rule attempts to advocate is avoidance of conflicts of interest. If your client asks you to help sue a company in which you happen to own 25 percent of the stock, you should consider directing the client to another attorney—preferably one who graduated from the Valdosta Legal Institute (certification pending).

Canon 6. A Lawyer Should Represent a Client Competently.

Anyone who would promulgate such a rule has incredible faith in the power of words—the kind of person who would put a "Do Not Steal" sign on the hubcaps of his Lincoln Continental in Manhattan.

Canon 7. A Lawyer Should Represent a Client Zealously Within the Bounds of the Law.

Although phrased as an order, this Canon constitutes a permit for what pragmatic lawyers do anyway—on behalf of paying clients. Lawyers need no reminder of the correlation between success in court and a client's willingness to pay legal fees.

HOW FAR
CAN YOU GO?

How far *can* you go in fulfilling Canon 7's mandate of zealous representation? Take the case of your client who is charged with stabbing someone in a dark alley. Can you ethically contend that he didn't actually stab the victim, but just happened to be holding the stiletto when the victim walked into it—backwards, 23 times?

Over the years, four tests have been formulated for measuring which arguments are acceptable, and which go too far:

(a) The "smell test." Also called the "cow flop" test. The most stringent of the four standards, this test precludes arguments that just don't smell right. Lots of arguments smell so bad that people in the courtroom will be checking the bottoms of their shoes.

(b) The "blush test." Also called the "red face test." If you can make a given argument without blushing, it passes. The stringency of this test, like that of the two tests below, varies depending on the shamelessness of the lawyer. Some lawyers can argue that their own mothers are virgins.

(c) The "gag test." Also called the "barf test." If you can utter a theory or alibi without gagging from the outrageousness of your words, it passes. This test is usually reserved for rich clients in bad trouble.

(d) The "lightning test." Also called the "wrath of God test." This is a test of extreme liberality, precluding only those arguments and theories so unsupportable that their very utterance is likely to cause lightning to strike you down as you speak. This test is applied by corporate takeover firms involved in tender offers.

COURTESY AMONG LAWYERS: "AFTER YOU, DOGBREATH"

The Code of Professional Responsibility requires lawyers to observe the highest standards of decorum in the courtroom. There they are expected to maintain utter civility, not only with respect to the judge (the so-called "bootlick imperative") but also with respect to each other.

This was not always true. Before the Code, lawyers were free to cast the harshest of aspersions on their opponents and their opponents' mothers.

Slurs like "dogbreath," "hairbag," and "mongrel scumsucker" were common.*

---

* Such coarseness was particularly common among lawyers who spent their undergraduate years in Hanover, New Hampshire.

One lawyer was heard to challenge his female opponent's sexual mores, admonishing her that "legal briefing" does not mean getting into the underpants of every lawyer in town. Another made the same point to a male opponent.

The Code has changed all that. Lawyers today consider themselves bold when firing shots such as "unfounded allegation," "dubious legal theory," and "hardly reasonable."

Not all post-Code lawyers are spineless and mealy-mouthed. One litigator was recently heard to comment that his opponent's personality was so bland that he carried a slice of Velveeta cheese in his wallet for identification. With good behavior he should be out in a few years.

XVIII.

How to Fix a Traffic Ticket

In any locality there are least three people, all city employees, capable of "fixing" a traffic ticket. These are (a) the policeman who was too busy measuring the distance between your car and the fire hydrant to care about rape and pillage in the streets, (b) the Cal Tech graduate who runs the computer that holds the ticket data, and (c) the judge who decides whether you should be sent to the Big House for not having enough change for the parking meter.

The first two of these can perform the fix simply by wiping your ticket off the books. Presto! It never happened. As for the judge, he can simply ignore it. He can decide in his wisdom that those three old coots his daughter ran over didn't have much time left in this world anyway.

If you want to fix a ticket, you first need to find the right person in the right place. With respect to the policeman or the computer jock, you either know him or you don't. Maybe the policeman lives next door. Maybe your brother, the black sheep of the family, went to Cal Tech with the computer jock.

What about the judge? You can find out with a few calls who'll be presiding in traffic court on the day you're scheduled to appear. But what do you do once you have his name? Call him up and say you're prepared to make him an offer he can't refuse? That would be extortion, and you don't want to get in so deep for a few lousy traffic tickets.

As with the policeman and the computer jock, you either know the judge or you don't. Judges usually fix tickets only for their buddies— the guys who let them win at golf each weekend, the guys

GOVERNMENT OF THE DISTRICT OF COLUMBIA

ON MON THE 6 DAY OF JUN 19 83 AT 1209 ☒ PM

VIOLATOR'S FULL NAME (LAST, FIRST, MIDDLE)

J. Earl Tirebiter ☒

STREET ADDRESS

SEX ?   HOME PHONE

CITY, STATE

DC RES   MO   DATE OF BIRTH
DAY   YEAR

OPERATORS PERMIT NO.   STATE

PLACE OF EMPLOYMENT

Unemployed   VEH MAKE VOLK   BODY 4

VEHICLE LICENSE NO.   989 9442 ☒   MO   YR   OTHER 84

LOCATION OF VIOLATION   2900 M ST

☒ N.W.   ☐ N.E.   ☐ S.W.   ☐ S.E.

MOVING VIOLATION
☐ ....TURN FROM WRONG LANE   ☐ DOT   ☐ SUPERIOR COURT
☐ RED LIGHT—T113   ☐ PEDESTRIAN VIOL.—P008
☐ FULL TIME & ATTN.—T013   ☐ NO PERMIT—T005
☐ FAIL TO YIELD ROW   ☐ SPEEDING:...........MPH
☐ ....SIGN VIOL   IN...........MPH ZONE
☐ RIGHT TURN ON RED—T116   ☐ OTHER.........................
☐ ACCIDENT   ☐ INJURY   ☐ ADMITTED   CCN: ....

PARKING VIOLATION   ☒ TOWING REQUESTED
39 ☒ RED METER (NO...18...)
55 ☐ NO PARKING ANYTIME   03 ☐ RESIDENTIAL PARKING
02 ☐ ALLEY   20 ☐ LESS 10' FIRE HYDRANT
07 ☐ IN BUS STOP/ZONE   31 ☐ IN LOADING ZONE
☐ LESS.........INTERSECTION   159 ☐ NO STAND, RUSH HOURS, AM
01 ☐ PARKING ABREAST   259 ☐ NO STAND, RUSH HOURS, PM
41 ☐ PRIVATE OR PUBLIC PROPERTY

☒ OTHER: Parking on elderly woman

SCHEDULED FINE OR COLLATERAL
☐ $5   ☒ $10   ☐ $15   ☐ $20   ☐ $25   ☐ $.........

OFFICER'S AVAILABILITY DATE
DAY OF ...., 19........ AT (TIME)...........

I personally observed or investigated the commission of the violation charged above and so state under my oath of office and under penalty of perjury.

ISSUER'S SIGNATURE   DEPT   ELEMENT BADGE NO.
Ullman   DOT HGB 766

I hereby acknowledge receipt of this notice of infraction and promise to pay or appear for a hearing within the time prescribed.

DATE 12/7/83   J. Earl Tirebiter   SIGNATURE

DOT FORM 51 DEC 81   COPY C

80885703 4

who give their kids free dental checkups, the guys who know about the plump redhead from Wellesley the judge has been fooling around with at those "judicial conferences" on the coast.

Enter the lawyer. The lawyer probably knows the judge. The judge may have been a former partner at his firm. Their kids probably break windows together.

The lawyer might also know the policeman or the computer jock. A lawyer with hustle familiarizes himself with the local courthouse, scurrying rodent-like about its darkest corridors, noting its corruptible elements.

If you don't know the right person to fix your tickets, there is probably a lawyer who does. And don't be embarrassed about asking the lawyers you know for help in this area—they're way past moral indignation.

But a bigger question than *how* to fix a ticket is whether, in business jargon,

the fix is cost-justified. (Note that morality never enters the picture.) The lawyer isn't going to use his contacts for a pittance. And the bureaucrats at the courthouse will charge whatever the market will bear. You don't want to find yourself paying $2,000 to fix $28 worth of tickets.

In some instances, such as where you're charged with reckless driving, driving while intoxicated, and negligent homicide by means of an automobile, you may be willing to pay whatever it takes. But then you're not talking about "fixing tickets"— you're talking about "beating a rap." That's a matter for another book.

XIX.

The Creative Art of Billing

Anyone who says lawyers aren't creative and imaginative hasn't seen a lawyer fill out his time sheets.

If you hope to succeed as a lawyer, it is essential to master the creative aspects of billing: as an associate, you can never tell partners how you really spent your time, and as a partner, you can never tell clients what they're really being billed for.

Even if you're a layman, it is important to understand the billing process—you'll still end up in hock to your lawyer, but you might get a tad more out of him for your money.

The following two time sheets illustrate the creative legal mind at its best.

What the Time Sheet Says:

CLIENT	ACTIVITY	TIME
1. T & L Goldberg, Inc.	Periodic review of active client litigation files	2 hours
	Phone conference with client Personnel re same	<u>1 hour</u> <u>3 hours</u>
2. PWCJR Oil Co.	Luncheon conference with client regarding outstanding matters, including lawsuit by employee labor union	<u>2 hours 20 minutes</u>
3. Ryan Leg Development Spa	Reviewing, editing and revising modified loan documents	<u>3 hours 55 minutes</u>

TOTAL TIME
BILLABLE TO CLIENTS   <u>9 hours 15 minutes</u>

How the Time Was Really Spent:

CLIENT	ACTIVITY	TIME
1. T & L Goldberg, Inc.	Thinking about client's new receptionist during morning jog	40 minutes
	Reading morning paper	45 minutes
	Rummaging through client files for name and number of client's new receptionist	30 minutes
	Getting coffee	15 minutes
	Calling client's new receptionist re dinner on Saturday night	50 minutes
		3 hours
2. PWCJR Oil Co.	Three-martini lunch with client at Chez St. Amand:	
	Discussing client's golf game and vacation in Barbados	120 minutes
	Telling ethnic jokes about employee–union officials	20 minutes
	(Client unaware he'd be billed for any of time)	2 hours 20 minutes

3. Ryan Leg Development Spa	Proofreading retyped loan documents	80 minutes
	Napping at desk	20 minutes
	Proofreading re-retyped loan documents	70 minutes
	Flirting with secretary	25 minutes
	Arranging for copying of re-re-retyped loan documents	40 minutes
		3 hours 55 minutes
TOTAL TIME BILLABLE TO CLIENTS		9 hours 15 minutes

"Airplanes and time zones are marvels of mankind . . . they've enabled me to bill 25 hours in a day."

DOUBLE BILLING
("Who says there are only 24 hours in a day?")

Perhaps the most ingenious device known to the law was conceived in response to the common misperception that there are only 24 hours in a day.

Double billing, or billing two clients for the same increment of time, occurs most frequently on trips. A lawyer flying, say, from New York to San Francisco to confer with two clients might bill the five hours of flight time to each. His rationale is that if he had made the trip for one client alone he'd have billed that client for all of the time—so why not bill all of it to each?

Some lawyers double bill as a matter of course. But none of them—not even the ones who triple bill and quadruple bill— acknowledge it publicly. They're greedy, not crazy. What they do is bury the double-billed item in the mountain of other items to be billed to the client in a month or two, and no one is the wiser.

The only way clients could monitor this practice would be to compare notes among themselves. They can't do that, of course. Antitrust laws forbid it. Antitrust laws arose about the same time as double billing.

XX.

Attorneys-at-Love: Dealing with Romantic Feelings Toward A Lawyer

YOU'VE HEARD THE STORIES. EVERYONE HAS. THEY'RE NOT PRETTY. MAYBE IT'S HAPPENED TO SOMEONE YOU KNOW. A FRIEND OR COLLEAGUE. MAYBE TO SOMEONE YOU LOVE— THAT'S WHEN IT REALLY HURTS.

What on earth could possess someone to become romantically involved with a lawyer? To most people such an occurrence seems about as likely as falling in love with a manhole cover. A prominent sociologist has compared the phenomenon to the pet rock fad that swept the country a few years ago—except, of course, for its tragic consequences.

What is to be done? Sadly, for those already involved, precious little *can* be done: anyone who has fallen in love with a lawyer is pretty far gone. The only real hope lies in prevention.

Prevention can best be accomplished by having nothing to do with lawyers except when it's absolutely necessary, like when you're about to be hauled off to jail. Even then you might want to think about it. You know, taste the food, talk to your prospective cellmate—give it a chance.

For most people, avoiding lawyers comes as naturally as breathing or, perhaps

219

"I am, among other things, a Juris Doctor."

more appropriate, squashing a bug. You see a lawyer and think, there but for the grace of God goes my dog. You feel the same contempt you feel for a drunk in the gutter— except the drunk might be pleasant company.

As difficult as it may be for most people to conceive of falling in love with a lawyer, a few seem to do it each year. What kind of perverse love are we talking about? It's difficult to describe, but if you've ever talked to a sailor who's been away at sea for ten or twelve months, you have an idea of the sort of unnatural craving involved. It's similar to the deranged mentality that students at certain schools in New Hampshire experience toward the end of a long winter. It can lead to anything.

Consider the case of Cathy X. X is not her real name. We'll call her Cathy. She was a bright 30-year-old nurse in Boston. She loved her work and entertained hopes of opening her own clinic someday. She also knew she wanted to fall in love, marry, and have a family. She didn't get many dates, though. She was a malignant dwarf. Also, she never had a tan, as she was an albino.

Enter Raymond Filbert (his real name—so what if a lawyer is publicly humiliated?), a conscientious associate at a large corporate law firm in Boston. They met by chance at a party. Raymond was trying to stab those little hot dogs you eat with toothpicks. Cathy was standing on her toes trying to reach the table. Their appetites were quickly diverted to each other. She drooled on his shoes, he drooled on her head.

WHAT TO BRING WITH YOU ON YOUR FIRST DATE WITH A LAWYER

If you're the reckless kind of person willing to date a lawyer, it's unlikely that you'll be prudent enough to equip yourself for the occasion in advance. You will realize your mistake soon enough, however—ten minutes, at the outside—and if at all possible you should pull over and grab the following helpful items:

1. Yellow legal pad.
2. Four packets of No-Doz.
3. English-Latin/Latin-English dictionary.
4. Lomotil.
5. C. Wright & A. Miller, *Federal Practice and Procedure* (1981).
6. Sony Walk-Man.
7. Cash.

Cathy knew from the outset that Raymond was a lawyer. It was a pool party, and everyone else was wearing bathing suits and sandals. Raymond was wearing a suit. Still, he was male, roughly speaking, and he seemed interested.

SPOTTING LAWYERS
OUT ON THE TOWN

In a better world, lawyers would never set foot out of their offices; they'd just live there—eating, sleeping, billing. Certain New York firms have attained this plateau.

Many lawyers still wander the streets, however, and running into one can ruin even a Saturday night. You're a friendly person. You enjoy meeting new people. But you have to draw the line somewhere. Hey, if you wanted to be bored you'd be back at work, or talking to your accountant.

If you spot a lawyer near you in a bar or restaurant, try spilling a drink on his trousers. The prospect of losing the crease will send him packing. If he gets aggressive about initiating conversation, call the authorities to have him physically ejected from the premises.

Don't worry about hurting his feelings. He's used to this type of treatment. Some lawyers go out in public *wanting* abuse, craving that mo-

ment of self-definition when they hit the sidewalk or the front grill of a passing vehicle.

What if you're not sure the person in question is a lawyer? When you're eleven bourbons into the evening, you may not be able to tell one from a foreigner who hasn't mastered standard English. Check him out with one of the following tests:

1. Ask him if he's a paralegal or a legal secretary. This suggestion will cause even the most practiced lawyer to flinch, redden and sputter (not to be confused with a Denver law firm by that name). Have him thrown out.

2. Assert that the legal profession should be regulated by a panel of laymen. This will trigger a strident attack on politicians, doctors and custom tailors. Have him thrown out.

3. Mention that you recently had your appendix removed, and you could swear you feel the outline of surgical clamps

still in your abdomen. Then stare into his face. If you're talking to a lawyer, his pupils will dilate, and saliva will appear around his lips. Have him thrown out.

4. State that you favor passage of no-fault insurance legislation. If he embarks on a polemic about the God-given right of every American to sue anybody for anything, have him thrown out.

5. Say that you've long considered briefcases and dictaphones to be emblematic of a truly advanced society. If he nods in agreement, have him thrown out.

If, despite your best efforts, a lawyer causes irreparable harm to your night on the town, don't just get depressed, chalking it off as another no-score inning in the game of life. Get even! Tell him you've got a potential client for him—and then give him the name of that life insurance salesman who's been bugging you for years. They deserve each other.

Can you find the lawyer in this picture?

"Let me get this straight . . . the perpetrator, a blonde Caucasian female, trespassed on your grounds, broke and entered into your dwelling, sat on your chairs, consumed your porridge, and slept in your beds . . . is that right?"

Their immediate infatuation yielded instantly to passion. They spent every night together for the next month. So inflamed was Cathy's ardor that she could overlook Raymond's insistence on wearing his three-piece suits to bed. "I think it's the vest," Raymond would say. "It makes me feel so masterful."

Cathy's enchantment soon turned to frustration. As time went on, Raymond began dragging himself home later and later. It reached the point that Cathy wouldn't know if Raymond was coming home at all; and when he did, usually around midnight, he would go straight to sleep (still wearing his suit, as mentioned).

For a while Cathy suspected Raymond was seeing another woman. Some of his sleep-talking sounded vaguely licentious, terms like "joinder of parties," "ejectment," and "post-trial briefs." As blind as love is, however, Cathy was able to make a realistic assessment of the chances of another woman becoming interested in Raymond, and she put that thought out of her mind.

Abstinence wasn't the worst of Cathy's problems

with Raymond. They didn't seem to communicate anymore. Raymond had taken to addressing Cathy in rude, condescending tones, which she knew he had picked up from the way senior partners at the firm addressed Raymond, and the way everyone at the firm addressed non-paying clients. Rather than simply talking with her, Raymond seemed to be lecturing her, and he had the strange habit of summarizing his argument at the outset and reserving three minutes for rebuttal.

The breakup wasn't long in coming. As lonely as Cathy was, she decided her pet goldfish would be better company, even though it had been floating at the top of the tank for a week.

Cathy had been pretty badly burned by this experience. She could take it, because albino dwarfs learn to take a lot, but she had learned her lesson the hard way and would never forget it: the only way to handle romantic feelings toward a lawyer is not to have any.

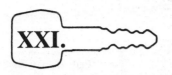

XXI.

You and Your Lawyer:
FINDING HIM, UTILIZING HIM, KEEPING HIM IN HIS PLACE

Sooner or later it happens to everybody. Your life is going along fine, the car is almost paid for, you just got a big promotion, your sex life is finally heating up—and suddenly disaster strikes. Your playful Great Dane—good

"It's frightening, I don't know anyone anymore who isn't a lawyer."

227

old Gaylord—dismembers a small child; you have a few drinks and on the way home decide to run that yellow light, only to notice too late the local sheriff's elderly mother stepping into the crosswalk; your wife finds some pink lace underwear in your glove compartment and doesn't buy your story about how much more comfortable you find them than your regular shorts during the summer heat.

Law books are full of such tales of disaster. What makes them disasters is that when they happen, you have to get a lawyer—Your Lawyer.

You've hoped against hope that you'd never have to do it. You've never felt comfortable around lawyers. You've never associated them with the good things in life.

But now there's no choice. Like appendicitis, your legal problem won't just go away. You have to *do* something about it—and you can't do it on your own.

The analogy to appendicitis is instructive: getting rid of your legal problem, like having your appendix removed, will be painful, costly (Your Lawyer will do a biopsy on your wallet), and will leave you slightly scarred.

But since it has to be done, you want it to be done right. This requires careful attention to certain points.

Selecting Your Lawyer

How do you go about the critical task of selecting Your Lawyer? Just let your fingers do the walking? Answer a television ad for one of those low-priced, polyester-vested hucksters who share walkup offices with the Acme Finance Company?

In law, as in life, you get what you pay for. You should choose Your Lawyer the same way you would a doctor —and you don't look for bargain basement prices when it comes to the person who's going to remove your adenoids, do you?

Get A Referral

A referral is your best bet. Ask your family friends, or minister. Do *not* ask your doctor. Doctors detest law-

DOCTORS v. LAWYERS
("Doc, I have this debenture that's been troubling me.")

Doctors and lawyers are notoriously hostile to one another. This seems strange at first because they're part of the same white collar professional world. They attended the same schools and have the same interests in Caribbean tax shelters. They're natural allies against the poor.

Nevertheless they're hostile. This is primarily because of jealousy on the part of lawyers. Consider job security: there will always be plenty of sick people, but every lawyer with a paying job knows there are 45 unemployed lawyers itching to replace him on a minute's notice.

It also has to do with wealth. The average doctor's income is literally twice that of the average lawyer.

Mainly, however, it has to do with prestige. Doctors have special license plates, for example, and get away with double-parking even if they're just visiting their accountant.

Similarly, doctors are called "Doctor," but nobody calls lawyers "Esquire." Sure, lawyers get "Attorney-at-law" on their embossed letterhead, but this is just a curiosity; you never hear of an Attorney-at-Plumbing or Attorney-at-Painting-Lines-on-Highways. And you certainly never hear of any professional basketball players called "Attorney J."

Doctors are called upon whenever there's an emergency. But has anyone ever stood up in a theater and cried, "Is there a lawyer in the house?"

Finally, it's common knowledge that while medical schools remain somewhat competitive, everybody in the country could get into *some* law school. Just think about the lawyers you know: some are bright enough, but how many will ever be picking up any prizes in Stockholm?

yers more than cancer, heart disease or socialized medicine. The mere idea that you're on the verge of hiring and *giving money* to a lawyer might induce your doctor subconsciously to leave scissors, clamps—even a Phillips head screwdriver—in your abdomen. (This is particularly troublesome if you're just in for a throat culture.)

The problem with the referral approach to finding a lawyer is that no one ever has anything good to say about his lawyer. Even your minister is likely to describe the lawyers he knows in language more frequently heard from dock workers. Still, if you can get a few names and numbers, you're on your way.

Do Comparative Shopping

Set up appointments with five or six lawyers, if you think you can stomach it. Remember that although the one you eventually hire will bill you for the precious time you squander in this first interview, the several you *don't* hire will have to absorb the loss. (If one of them tries to hit you up for a couple of hundred dollars anyway, feel free to light a cigar with his bill—it'll never be worth his while to sue you for that amount.)

Prepare for Your Appointment
("Just the facts, Ma'am")

Okay. So you've set up your first appointment with a lawyer. Relax. If the guy turns out to be even worse than you expected, you still have hundreds more to choose from. Console yourself with the thought that no matter how bad things are, at least *you're* not a lawyer.

As the appointment day draws near, collect your thoughts. Figure out what it is you want Your Lawyer to do for you. You're going to pay through the nose for it. You might as well get your money's worth.

When you arrive at Your Lawyer's building, go straight to the office directory on the wall of the lobby and note four things: how many lawyers are in Your Lawyer's firm; how many floors in the

"Legal questions are never cut and dried, Mr. Snead. The fact that you're paying through the nose for our services doesn't mean we can guarantee results."

building are occupied by Your Lawyer's firm; how many floors are there between the floor on which Your Lawyer is located and the highest floor occupied by the firm; how close to the top of the building is the firm. These trifling facts, although of no consequence whatsoever to most people, are highly important to Your Lawyer. In dealing with him, it is important that you understand the thoughts that dominate his waking hours, even as his time is being billed to you.

Next go up to Your Lawyer's floor, and ask the receptionist to let him know you are there. Do not be put off by having to wait longer than you do when renewing your license plates. Be happy that at least you do not have to stand in line. In the waiting area, savor the luxury of filthy but thoughtfully spent lucre: the Persian rugs, the exotic plants, the Renaissance masterpieces adorning the walls. Try not to think about who's paying for them.

Stay Cool

Eventually a secretary will arrive to escort you to the inner sanctum, where you will finally cast eyes upon the curiosity who may become Your Lawyer. Keep your wits about you now. Take note of various points of manner, such as whether he steps forward to greet you openly, or conducts the interview from behind his desk (so that you cannot be sure he is wearing trousers); whether he asks his secretary to hold all calls, or subjects you to interruptions from his other clients' parole officers.

Above all, do not be intimidated. Ask him where he went to law school and how high he graduated in his class. Make him explain the difference between herringbone and tweed. Remember: he's not Your Lawyer yet.

Discuss the Fee

An essential matter for you to raise on this first visit is the fee. Lawyers never bring it up on their own. They can be strangely cryptic in this regard, purporting to disdain the subject of fees as too crass for discussion.

Do not be taken in by this pose. In this regard, as in others, lawyers resemble ladies of the night: the most charming can be the most vicious when it comes to collecting their fees. Recall that fee collection time is one of the rare occasions when a lawyer becomes free to violate the much touted sanctity of the attorney-client privilege.

Reject evasive answers. You don't want to discover too late that Your Lawyer's casual reference to "my standard rate" means $300 per hour. Neither should you rest easy with the assurance,

"Oh, I think we can work out something that will be mutually satisfactory." Hey, if you weren't desperate, you wouldn't be paying him *anything*.

Be prepared to have to work for an answer. He might attempt full-scale diversionary tactics:

> "That's a good question, and I'm glad you had the presence of mind to raise it at the outset. Too often, I think, lawyers are so busy striving to advance their clients' interests that they lose sight of these kinds of questions and neglect to establish any true understanding—or what could be called a meeting of the minds—as to how it will all shake out in the long run. Why, I recall one case out in California . . ."

"I find it helps to remind myself that the client is the one in trouble . . . nobody's talking about sending me to jail!"

When this romp through ir-relevance terminates, repeat your question. Do so again and again, until either you get an answer or the cleaning people come in to vacuum and turn off the lights.

You Call the Shots

The basic rule in utilizing Your Lawyer is: *he* works for *you,* not vice versa. You pay the bills; you call the shots.

Early on in the relation-ship you will find Your Law-yer telling you what you can and can't do, or what, ac-cording to him, you *have* to do. Nip this in the bud. Tell him what *you* want, and if he can't make it happen, let him know you're prepared to take your business down the road. You will be surprised at how quickly he will decide, after a little additional research, that what you wanted seems to be possible after all.

Monitor His Work

Monitor closely the work on your case, contract, or whatever. Ask for periodic, detailed statements of ac-count. If Your Lawyer gets the idea that you aren't too worried about the size of the bill, it will expand in ways you couldn't imagine. It will manage to take on expensive dinners, exotic travel, pe-ripheral research that would have been done anyway for other clients—things that A.T. & T. may not mind sub-siding, but you do.

You don't want to go overboard with the monitor-ing. Even a twenty-second phone conversation with Your Lawyer can cost you as much as dinner for eleven at an expensive restaurant—that's *with* wine.

The fact is that anything Your Lawyer does for you starts the meter running. It doesn't matter if he's just sending you a copy of a brief or a recent statement of ex-penses. It doesn't matter if he's just *thinking* about send-ing you a copy of a brief or a recent statement of expenses. If he's doing anything that so much *reminds* him of you, you'll be billed for the time.

Keep Him in Perspective

It's important to remem-ber that Your Lawyer is,

after all, only a lawyer. He is not a psychotherapist, a minister, or even a friend. That you come to him in trouble, and that you tell him intimate details of your life, does not alter the basic fact that his interest in you is commercial.

Your Lawyer may sound personally interested in the details of your gall bladder operation; you may appreciate his expressions of outrage as you describe your wife's infidelity, or your husband's violent tendencies as he reaches his sixth martini every evening. But remember that with each word you utter, Your Lawyer's meter is clicking away. If that meter isn't running, Your Lawyer isn't listening.

Legal Glossary
(LATIN AND OTHER FOREIGN TONGUES)

Accord and Satisfaction— 1. Resolution of a claim for breach of contract, whereby the parties agree to alter the original terms of the contract. 2. Carnal indulgence in the rear seat of a Japanese automobile.

Ambulance Chasing—A client development practice common among personal injury lawyers.

Amicus Curiae—Latin, "Friend of the curious." The person who works at the information desk in federal courthouses.

Belts and Suspenders—Refers to provisions in legal documents that are duplicative or redundant, just as belts and suspenders are sartorially redundant on all but the most interesting physiques.

Bench Warrant—A guaranteed seat in court.

Codicil—1. An addition to or modification of a will. 2. A lower undergarment worn by 17th century French soldiers.

Common Pleas—1. The title of certain courts of limited jurisdiction in medieval England and modern Pennsylvania. 2. Any of various excuses for non-performance of marital requests, such as "Not tonight, Dear—I have trust indenture."

Contributory Negligence—In Manhattan, the doctrine that anyone who leaves his car guarded by less than a battalion of U.S. Marines is as much to blame as the person who stole it.

237

Damnum Absque Injuria—Latin, "Loss without injury." A polite reference to the retirement of nonproductive senior partners. *See* Rule Against Perpetuities.

Egress—In real property law, an exit. In general, a way out, which is what every lawyer wants.

Ex Lax—Latin, "From the lawyer." Refers to memos, briefs and other work product of lawyers.

Fee—1. In real property law, an unrestricted estate in land. 2. A term whose loud utterance—"Fee?"—constitutes the lawyers equivalent for "Is there a doctor in the house?"

Force Majeure—In contract law, an irresistible force, including hurricanes, floods, wars, and the smell of winos in subways.

Habeas Corpus—Latin, "You've got a body." A conversation opener at discotheques in ancient Rome.

Hung Jury—A divided jury, *i.e.,* one in which the jurors cannot reach agreement on the question of the defendant's guilt or innocence. Ironic term, because if the jury is hung, the defendant isn't.

Illegitimi Non Carborundum—Latin, "Don't let the bastards get you down." 1. The motto of lawyers who deal with the Internal Revenue Service. 2. H.U.B.

In Loco Parentis—Latin, "In the place of a parent." Mexican, "Crazy Momma."

Last Clear Chance—1. In tort law, the doctrine that liability (as for an automobile collision) should rest with the person who had the last opportunity to avoid the collision. 2. In general, the moment before taking the LSATs.

Layman—What lawyers call the person they screw.

Learned Hand—1. A prominent 20th century judge on the United States Court of Appeals. 2. A famous 16th century Turkish eunuch. Not related to Learned Tongue.

Learned Hand, Chief Judge of the United States Court of Appeals for the Second Circuit.

Litigation—A basic right in the American system of justice, which offers every aggrieved person his decade in court.

Parachuter—Someone who enters a law firm laterally, *i.e.,* after working somewhere else, rather than coming in straight from law school. Invariably loathed by those beneath him in seniority.

Plead the Fifth—Often confused with alcohol-related excuses for tabletop dancing at office Christmas parties, to "plead the fifth" is to assert one's right under the fifth amendment of the U.S. Constitution to refuse to answer questions if the answers might be self-incriminating—*e.g.,* "What did you do with the corpse?"

Pro Bono Publico—Latin, "For the public good." Refers to legal services performed without charge, usually for ingrates.

Rainmaker—A lawyer whose compensation bears no relation to his legal skills.

Res Ipsa Loquitur—Latin, "It won't stop talking." A legal defense to the crime of killing parrots and myna birds.

Settlement—A device by which lawyers obtain fees without working for them.

Stare Decisis—"To stare decisively." In criminal law, refers to the process by which an assault victim indicates which of the suspects in a lineup he believes to have been his assailant.

Usufruct—1. In real property law, the right to enjoy the fruits of land owned by someone else. 2. An Italian gesture of contempt.

Watered Stock—1. In securities law, stock issued for an amount less than its par value. 2. Bloated cattle.

Once you've finished *The Official Lawyer's Handbook,* you're better prepared for a legal career than any sad product of Yale or Columbia. Unlike the graduates of conventional legal institutes—indebted to the hilt and helpless prey to the experienced vultures of the law—you're ready for clients! Don't be modest about the insights you've acquired. Tear out the diploma on the following page and display it prominently in your office. You've earned it.

Lawperosus Parrissus

Gallia Est Divis In Tres Partes.

Illegitimi Non Carborundum.

GLUTEUS MAXIMUS CHASERIBUS AMBULANCI

Let it be known that _____

having successfully completed the curriculum

Bull Crappus Slingus ad Nauseum

and being thereby entitled to the degree of

Juris Doctor

is accordingly awarded said degree with all the rights, privileges and immunities thereunto appertaining; in witness whereof we have caused our corporate seal to be here affixed on this _____ day of _____, in the year of our Lord one thousand nine hundred and _____,

D. Robert White

Chief Solicitor